A History of Cwmgwyn
1900–2000

A History of Cwmgwyn 1900–2000
a chapel and its people

by
Clarice Thomas

Cwmgwyn Press

CWMGWYN PRESS
The Stores & Post Office, Felindre,
Knighton, Powys LD7 1YN

First published by Cwmgwyn Press in 2005
Copyright © text Clarice Thomas 2005
Copyright © illustrations as acknowledged

All rights reserved. No part of this publication
may be reproduced, stored in a retrieval system,
or transmitted, in any form or by any means,
electronic, mechanical, photocopying, recording
or otherwise, without the prior permission,
in writing of the publisher

ISBN
0 9551582 0 6
978 0 9551582 0 9

Set in Times and New Baskerville by Logaston Press
and printed in Great Britain by
Biddles Ltd, King's Lynn

Contents

	page
Acknowledgements	vii
Map showing most of the houses mentioned	ix
Introduction	1

The Drovers	2	Lost houses above Cwmgwyn	113
Ty-un-nos	5	The Prysg	115
Yrchen, Yr-ychen or Iyrchyn	9	Panty-Beudy	117
Cider House	11	Tynllwyn	120
Cwmgwyn Chapel	14	Llethrau Cottage	122
The Ddol Farm, Cwmgwyn	33	The Llethrau	123
Walk Mill	36	Medwaledd	127
Dolfrynog	37	Tyn-y-Cwm	130
The Culvert	41	High Park	135
Bwlch-y-llyn	44	Slate House	137
The Waen	47	The Lluest	139
Windy Hall	67	Persandy	142
Fiddlers Green	70	The Turgey	143
Lower Fiddlers Green	76	The Oaks	143
Brickhouse or Bryn-mawr	78	Newcwm	145
Friesland	81	Hope's Castle	149
The Gravel	81	The Bog	152
Hafod Fadog	83	Shell Heath	154
Cwmgwyn Hall	85	The Trefoil	154
Tynllidiart	86	Coventry	155
Little House	87	The Slopes & Cork Hall	155
Butterwell	96	Wisdom Castle & Bright's Farm	156
Lower Voil, Blaen-Voil & Blaen-cwm-Voil	100	Penybank & Cwmgarthen	156
		Dolfryn	159
Blaen-Nanty	105	The Ddol, Llanbadarn Fynydd	161
Springfield	109	Gwenlas	164
The Garn	110	Felindre Village Life	167

Index   177

Cwmgwyn Chapel

by
Mrs. Joan Lewis, The Garn

1. A cute little Chapel
   By the name of Cwmgwyn,
   It stands in the valley
   With the hills looking in.
   Of stone it is built
   And oil lamps for light,
   For families to worship
   In the morn and at night.

2. For miles they would walk
   With their children so small
   To this dear little Chapel;
   There was welcome for all.
   To the sermons would listen,
   Sing hymns and they pray
   For the love of the Saviour
   On the Sabbath day.

3. When the service was ended
   Again they would roam
   Along the rough pathways,
   So pleased to be home.
   A rest they would take
   And the Bible would read,
   Before they sat down
   To a jolly good feed.

4. But the years have rolled by
   And the future looks bright,
   For now in the Chapel
   Electric light.
   Repairs have been made,
   New windows and doors
   And warm cosy carpet
   All over the floors.

5. This staunch little Chapel
   With its members so few,
   The doors they keep open,
   What else can they do?
   Some meetings are special
   Bringing crowd from afar,
   But now they don't walk
   They drive their own car.

6. So peaceful it stands,
   For all people to see
   But still as it was
   And ever will be.
   A place where to worship
   And sing praises within,
   This dear little Chapel
   By the name of Cwmgwyn.

Acknowledgements

That is some of the history of the upper reaches of the River Teme, for I still hear things which I have not included and sometimes I think I should have re-write some — but time is passing too quickly, so this had to be the end. When I started, over four years ago, I said I would finish it — if I lived long enough! Well, I am still alive and the book is here.

I can hear some of the older folk saying — 'ah, but you binna right there' — well I apologise, but I have tried my best. My information has come from talking to people, the census forms and books, although very little has been written about the top end of the valley.. I hope some of you will enjoy reading the book — or at least parts of it. I think some of the photographs will bring a smile to a few faces.

I have so many people to thank who have helped me in so many ways, but I feel there are a few who have gone 'the extra mile', especially these modern folk who can use computers, and type up all the many pages I have written, and then put it all on a 'floppy disc'. It was only recently that I discovered what a floppy disc was, (and even now I hear that these discs have been superseded by an even smaller, and I would think more complicated, piece of equipment). So special thanks to Sheila Dewis, Mrs. Caroline Lloyd and my grandchildren, Alan and Vicky Thomas. Also to Myfanwy Evans and Richard Turner, who tried so hard to teach me to type and print out my own work. Sorry Richard, but I am too old or too stupid, although I told myself that I was too busy!

Then many thanks to folk who have let me borrow photographs, some very old, so that I can use them in the book and maybe make it more interesting. Also thanks to Mrs. Jayne Harris who has taken photographs of the children on the stage at the chapel over the past few years. It is good to see the children willing to go on stage and sing and recite, and I am very grateful to the parents for bringing them there. Thanks too, to Vicky, Kate and Nick, who have these up-to-date cameras to take photographs.

I must also thank the folk who have spent time talking to me, especially some of the older folk who still have wonderful memories. I think, in the days before the telly, we used to sit and talk to our parents and older relations, and some of us can still remember the things they told us!

Thanks too, to a few who have actually written their own history, and some who have written notes for me to use. And lastly thanks to a very few who, at the last minute, have written their history since moving into a local home. It has been like trying to 'get blood out of a stone', but we've got there just in time. And now, many thanks to all who may read it.

From left to right. Back row: David Morris, Keith Thomas, Frances Morris, Joan Lewis, Megan Savage, Ken Price, Brian McCann, John Stephens

Second row from back: Mrs. Baker, Margaret Stephens, Alwena Stephens, Margaret Lewis, Cliff James, Bill Watson

Second row from front: Mable Stanfield, Clarice Thomas, Tilda Price, Gwyneth McCann, Nelda Foster, Mary Wilding

Front row: Marc Thomas, Hannah Meredith, Frances Williams

Cwmgwyn Baptist Chapel Choir at Knighton Baptist Chapel, 4th July 1998

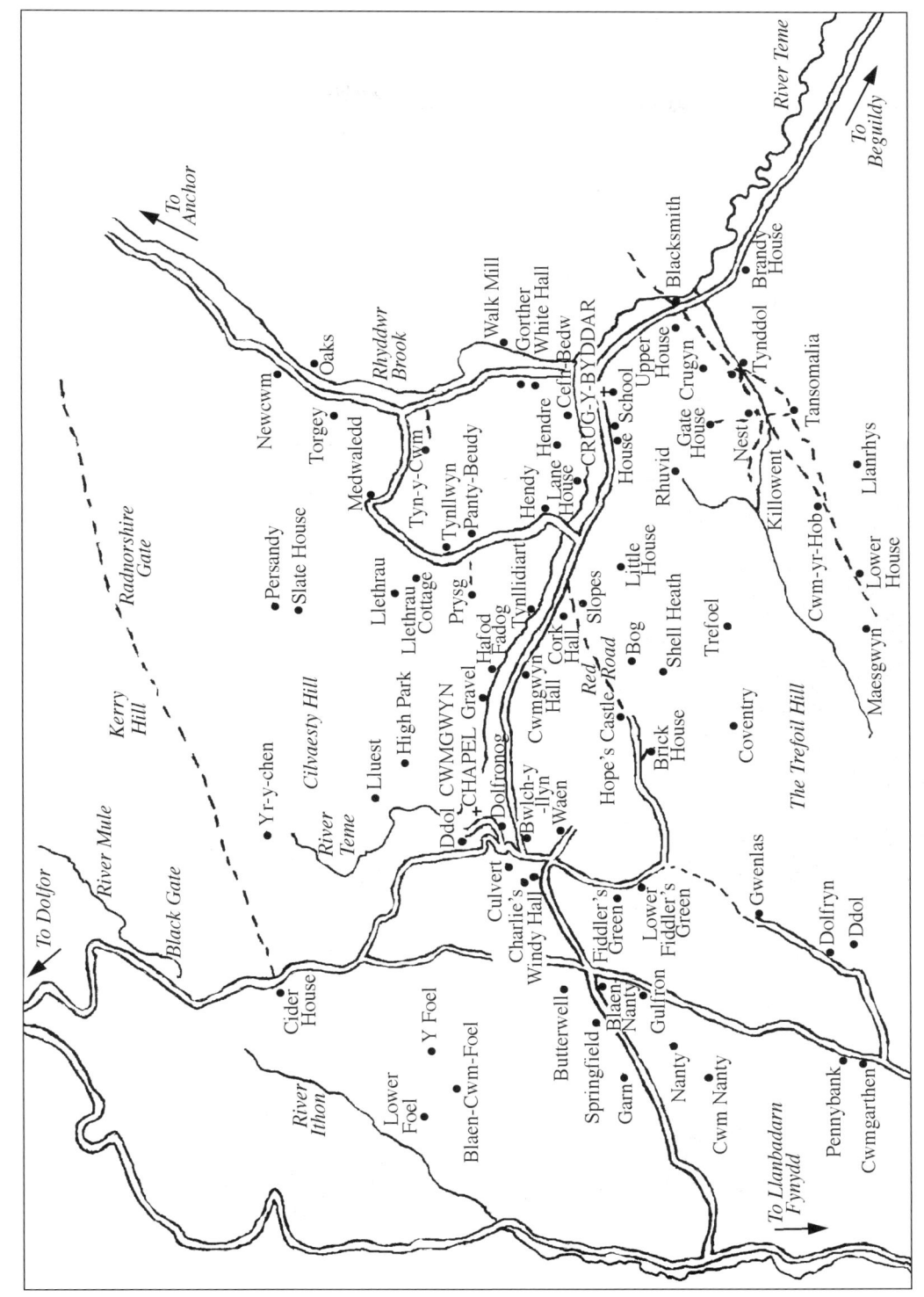

Map of the area showing the location of the houses most commonly mentioned

Passing Through

We are only passing through, passing through this way.
   So let us try to do our very best from day to day.
Doing everything for loved ones — while they're here.
   Let us prove the heart's affection, while we have them near.

We are only passing through — and life is very short.
   So strive to make the most of it — in word and deed and thought
To smooth a path for others and to cause them no distress
   Giving only Joy and Comfort, Help and Happiness.

Always keep your promises — no matter what it costs.
   You can't patch up a friendship once the confidence is lost.
Do your duty so that none can ever point to you
   And say — you failed or faltered in the task you had to do.

Life upon this little Earth is just an episode
   A journey, and we pass but once along this bit of road.
So — do to others as you would that they should to you
   You will not come this way again, you are only passing through.

The author on the day that the first wedding was witnessed at Cwmgwyn — that of John Stephens and Mair Thomas in May 2001

Introduction

Some years ago, a Mr. Brian Draper came up to this area to research the River Teme from its source to where it joins the Severn near Worcester. Later, he came to Felindre Village Hall to give a talk on his findings. He also brought slides, and I was so impressed that I thought — why not write the history of the top end of the River Teme and the many homesteads around it. Well, why not indeed? That was a few years ago now and I am still up at the top end of the Teme and struggling. But if I live long enough, I'll get there.

The source of the Teme is near an almost derelict little house called Yrchyn or Yr-Ychen, which translated from the Welsh means 'the oxen'. It is right out on the open hill, with no road and no amenities, and has been empty for many years. But it was put on the market last year and sold to a family from Telford, so maybe there will be life up there again.

To find out about this home I got hold of the census return for 1891, the latest one available at the time. This would enable me to find out who lived there, and how they made a living. Well, I can tell you, I've had a surprise! To think that I lived up at the Waen for nearly twenty-five years, and knew nothing much about what had gone on in that area over the last hundred years.

So started my search for anything and everything I could find out about the many little homesteads up and around the source of the River Teme. I wondered why so many little houses (and they were small) were built up on the hills and moors, and in such out of the way places, often very difficult places to get to.

Well, I had to go just a little further up the hill above Yrchyn, across the main road from Knighton to Newtown and there was a rather large and, once again, derelict farmhouse — namely, Cider House — and now I see that here was the answer to many of my 'wonderings'.

This turned out to be a very important 'resting place' for the drovers in the 18th and 19th centuries, and even possibly before that. It was the drovers who brought work and money with them and these were, and still are, two of the main factors needed to make any area grow and prosper. So I started off very enthusiastically, asking questions and handing out questionnaires, especially to the older folk living around, but I'm afraid I had little response. The only way, I have found, is to go to their homes with pen and notepad and ask questions — and even that I have found difficult. I get so interested and engrossed in their stories, that I forget all about taking notes! I have tried taking a tape recorder with me, but I find that people seem to be very conscious of it being there, and do not speak so freely. Quite often some of the older folk will say to me, 'Ah, but you remember him', but I don't, because we didn't move into the area until 1956, so I am a comparative newcomer and should not really be the person writing this book. 'Fools rush in where angels fear to tread' has come to mind often.

However, I have tried to get some of the history of our area — if for no other reason than to prove something to a foreign lady, who came out to see me about a grant to help with costs of producing this book. She said, as she left, that she would go up to the Cwmgwyn area to look around and would let me know by post whether the application was successful. When the letter arrived, the answer was negative as 'I feel that there are not enough people living there to warrant a grant.' Well, of course, there are not many people living up there now but it was a very busy area a hundred years ago, and I wanted to try to record that. Her response was enough to get my hackles up and make me even more determined — grant or no grant — to write about the history of the past one hundred years. I have had a few knocks along the way and many times thought of packing it all in — but that foreign lady has kept me going!

The Drovers

Wales, with its mountains and valleys has always been a good ground for stock — the sheep on the hills and the cattle in the valleys. Over the centuries, even back as far as the Middle Ages, these animals have provided the Welsh farmers with a good livelihood, especially if they could get them across to the English markets. In those days, there were no roads, so no transport. The only way was to walk the animals over the rough roads and tracks, and so started the need for the drovers. These would be strong, healthy men who were willing to rough it on the journey across to England, which would often take weeks. Their pay was said to be little better than that of farm labourers, but maybe a little more exciting.

As the Welsh meat, especially the Welsh Black cattle, and the sweet mountain lamb, became more popular in England, so the need for drovers increased. It is said that the gentlemen of England in their large country houses soon acquired a taste for 'the roast beef of old England' which was actually often the Welsh Black cattle from Wales.

As the the trade between Wales and England grew, so the drovers began to become more organised. Some of the men who had been droving for years and knew the ups and downs of the job became Master Drovers. They would ride a pony and have their corgi dog by their side, along with around twelve strong, fit men on foot to drive a herd consisting of up to three or four hundred head of cattle.

There were many routes into England, and each Master Drover had his own. The route which brought work and money into the area around the source of the River Teme — the Cwmgwyn area — was the route from North Wales, via Machynlleth, Staylittle, Llanidloes, and Llandinam and then over the hill to Cider

House. Here they would rest for a day, or longer, and then down into England via the Anchor. It is said that in the 17th century, three thousand cattle left via this route for the English markets, and by the 18th century that number had doubled, and later trebled.

The Master Drover had much planning to do before setting out on these long journeys. He had to organise collecting points and find out the numbers to be taken. Then each 'resting place' had to be informed of when they would arrive, so that there would be fodder and pastures for the stock, accommodation for himself at an inn or farmhouse, and warm barns for the drovers. Then, most importantly, a blacksmith near at hand to re-shoe the cattle. These needed new shoes or 'cues' at most of the resting places, and strong local men were needed to catch and floor the cattle and tie their legs up — all four together — ready for the blacksmith to re-shoe them. Safe 'pounds' or paddocks for the stock overnight, or often longer, were also needed. The animals and the drovers needed rest, and as there were often brigands and, in the early days, wolves roaming the hills, the local men were also needed to guard the stock overnight and allow the drovers and animals to rest. All this planning and organising had to be done without telephones, and post when it did come into use was not very reliable so I would think that most of the organising and planning would be done while they were returning from their previous trip.

The Cider House used to put on entertainment for the drovers — music and dancing, sometimes an organised boxing match between the drovers and local lads and, of course, plenty of food and cider in the red-roofed shed near the road, which was called The Drovers' Inn. This meant that girls and women would be needed for the catering, so many locals would benefit from the drovers' stop.

The movement of stock from Wales into England continued without much hassle from anyone until King Edward VI and Queen Elizabeth required the Master Drover to be issued with an annual licence. Amongst the criteria that had to be met were that the Master Drover had to be married, a house owner and at least thirty years old. Indeed, Master Drovers became highly respected men, to whom large sums of money were entrusted for transit to and from London and other markets. One such, named Evan Davies, was twice made the High Sheriff of Radnorshire in the late 17th century.

Archie the Drover with Turk

Later on, when the non-conformists became very strong in Wales, the drovers were threatened with 'eternal damnation' as being amongst those who worked on Sundays and in 1845 three drovers in Knighton were fined £1 each with 8s. 6d. costs for driving animals through the town on the Sabbath day. Thus, Sunday became a 'day of rest' for all drovers. Later again, the tollgates caused them trouble, and at the end of the 19th century the railways came and these really did sound the knell for the drovers. From then on there was a steady decline in the movement of stock by foot across Wales and into England.

Towards the end of the drovers' wonderful life, they would also include sheep, pigs and geese as well as the cattle. Mrs. Phoebe Reynolds remembers when she grew up in the Llanbister area some eighty years ago, that the ladies round about would knit socks for the geese to wear on their journey. Her grandmother lived at the Turnpike, so would be involved with the drovers and their stock. Also, Jack Davies, Penybank, told me that the geese from the Cwmgwyn area — and there were many — would often walk to Newtown Market and they would be fitted with shoes made of tar. The tar would be warmed up in a shallow tin and when it had cooled down, the geese had their feet dipped into it, then held up off the ground until the tar had set. This was done to stop the geese getting blisters on their feet.

One lady, Mrs. Elsie Brick of Felindre, remembers that when she was a child at Stoney Pound, there would be great excitement when they knew the drovers were coming. The children would all sit on the side of the road, waiting, and what a noise as the animals came nearer — mooing and baaing! The women would bring out cups of tea for the men, and then they would be on their way over to the Clun area. This would be in the mid to late 1920s.

Here is another of our local characters — 'Green Wellies'. Richard Coyle used to travel around this area from Abbey-Cwm-Hir to Felindre, asking only for food and a bed in a barn. His family in Ireland had been informed in the 1940s that he was missing, presumed killed in the war. He is buried in Llanbadarn churchyard, and the Dolithon Choir with the Rev. Father J. Clarke arranged the service, and many of his former friends attended his funeral. Jack Penybank made a wooden cross and the choir put an old boat filled with wild flowers on his grave

Even after this time we hear of a few individual drovers, living rough around the hill-farming areas. I can remember Archie and his faithful dog, Turk, living around Llanddewi. He would sometimes go to my husband's home, Castlepren, and help them to walk their stock to Penybont market. His pay would be a warm bed in a hay-barn for a few nights, good food and a small amount of cash. Too much, and he would spend it all in the local and be difficult to manage.

When the organised drovers' work had come to an end, it was a sad day for many of these people living in the little homesteads on the hill. There lives had to change dramatically in order to survive. Many sold their little houses with its plot of land, usually to a neighbouring farmer, and with their small amount of money set out to find work elsewhere — often down to the coalmines, or some to the Midlands where factories were setting up and needed workers. A few of these little houses are still being lived in, but many are just a few stones and a memory.

Ty-un-nos

Ty-un-nos houses, or House in one night/Morning surprise or simply 'Clod' houses (so-called round here) played a big part in rural life especially on the rough moorlands and hills above Felindre. This land was Crown land, so was not owned by anyone local, although farms touching this land were allowed a 'turn-out' onto it, the amount of stock depending on how much of their land was touching the Crown land.

These *ty-un-nos* houses had certain rules that must be adhered to if the builders were to keep their new homes. Building had to start after sunset and a roof had to be on and smoke coming out of the chimney by sunrise next morning. They were allowed to fence a small patch of ground around it, or dig a ditch — again during that night. I have read that this patch had only to be an 'axe throw' from the house in all directions, but some of these smallholdings must have had some very strong men around to throw an axe that far.

There was quite a lot of planning to be done beforehand. These farmhands were not stupid, and when they had worked on farms for several years they would have acquired many skills with their hands. Also, they were conscientious workers who wanted a better life for themselves and their family, and this was an ideal opportunity to have your own home for just about next to nothing.

Several friends and family would get together and have the materials and tools needed hidden away in a quarry or a clump of trees or bushes near where the house was to be built. Some would also have had a door and window ready, made by the local carpenter, but no one was allowed to help him during the night.

Often these houses would be very small — only one room up and one room down. What great excitement it must have been for the farm-workers whose lives were otherwise very hard and dull, to see that smoke rising in the early morning. How some of us would love to have this opportunity today. The houses were then

The Old House, Bwlch-y-llyn. I think this is a good example of a Ty-un-nos.
It was lived in right up to the late 1970s

named and registered, and then they were theirs. Around here some of these names were very 'grand', for example Hope's Castle, Cork Hall and Windy Hall, up near Cwmgwyn. After the houses had been registered, the owners were allowed to improve and enlarge them. Sometimes they would build another house on their patch and turn the first into a barn or cowshed, but the second house was usually only two up and two down — still very small for the size of most families. And so with their small patch of ground and their few animals out on the open hill, they could be just about self-supporting, especially if the man could get a part-time job or casual work — and there was always plenty of this around a drovers' route.

I have also been told that some of the farmers encouraged their workers to build, particularly on wet and boggy ground. When the wet patch had been fenced in, the farmer's sheep could not graze there and so, hopefully, not get the 'fluke worm', which is very harmful to sheep. Possibly the Bog and Shell Heath were two of these small dwellings.

Having seen some of these 'small' enclosures, I think these folk were adding to their patch each year, either by moving the fence further out onto the hill or by just adding another field now and again.

It has been claimed that these small enclosures played a considerable part in the reclamation and improvement of the higher land in Radnorshire, and they certainly helped to make the Cwmgwyn area come alive, especially the little chapel. During the early days of the 20th century, this chapel would be full to overflowing, and if you wanted a seat for a Sunday 6.30 p.m. service, you needed to be there by six o'clock.

In 1905, the Earl of Birkenhead had a law passed in Parliament that no more Crown land was to be built on or fenced in, so that was the end of the little clod houses. By then, however, many of these little homesteads had enough land and a good solid house in which to live quite comfortably. Today, we would have great difficulty in trying to live in such houses, especially with no road, no bathroom or running water, no electricity and no transport. But they knew no other, and so were happy.

In the latter part of the 19th century the Radnorshire County Council was formed, and they began to take an interest in our roads and bridges. In 1890 the Council bought two scraping machines to scrape the mud off the roads and help keep them in order. Before their appearance, each farmer put in his four to six hours per year, with his horse and wagon, laying fresh stone on top of the mud, and all workmen had to give several hours to level the stone. Back in those days, and for many years before, travellers were warned when they reached Beguildy that the road to Newtown was not passable for pony and trap beyond Felindre. They were advised to go back to Knighton, then on to Clun.

In 1899 the Council bought its first steamroller, and in 1920 a bigger and heavier roller, but these rollers could not be used on the roads above Felindre. By the early 1930s the council had made a road up the hill beyond the chapel, and it was passable but not good. Then in the late 1930s this road began to give the council cause for concern. On the very top it had been built too near the edge, and there was a very steep drop down to the bottom of the narrow Teme valley. The council had to move the road a few yards further across the moor away from the edge, and when it was finished they brought a 13 ton steam roller out to make a good surface. One of our senior local men remembers that they had to make a hasty retreat, as the roller was beginning to sink. So our country roads, especially in these hilly areas, were still a problem, and remained so until well into the 20th century, when I have read that one of our senior Radnorshire Council men became friendly with a descendant of John McAdam who had invented, many years before, a wonderful method of road-making. Both these men had sons in the same University, and the families became good friends; and so it was that our Radnorshire roads began to be macadamised.

The Council now needed men to help improve the roads and then to maintain them, and so many of the men living up on the hills, and especially the older men, became roadmen. They continued to work on our roads right up to the end of the 20th century, when our Councillors, in their wisdom, decided we could manage without them — a very sad day!

However, even before then, indeed as from the mid-1940s, after the war, when the drovers were long gone and with them the casual work and the ready money, the people from these little homesteads up in the hills began to move away to look for work. Many of these little houses with their small piece of land were sold, usually to a neighbouring farmer, and the family moved away, taking their small amount of money with them to help them to set up home elsewhere. Quite often it was back to the coalmines, but also the Midlands were setting up new factories so some went there to find work. Their little houses up on the hills were used as winter shelter for the animals, and hay and straw was stored up in the bedrooms.

Even so ome of these little houses are still standing and have had people living in them all through the 20th century — Hope's Castle, Tynllwyn and Llethrau Cottage and, of course, the Ddol just above the chapel started life as a little *ty-un-nos* but has been improved and enlarged several years ago. Then there are Dolfrynog and Little House, two little *ty-un-nos* homes bought by city folk who have spent a lot of time and money enlarging these little homes, but have kept the original little house, which now blends in with the extensions.

There are even a couple of *ty-un-nos* homes which had been turned into cattle sheds, but which are now turned back into homes for people to live in. Llanmadoc is one in the Beguildy area and The Prysg is the other up in the Cwmgwyn area. This house was sold to the Stephens family many years ago and has been a shelter for the animals, but when Alwena (née Stephens) married Charles Campbell in 2001, they decided to turn it back into a house and make it their home.

Some of the occupants of these houses found employment in the forestry and timber industries when these became active around these hilly areas, but like the roads, these has now just about ceased to exist, so finding work in these isolated areas is still a problem.

Today, the farmers around do not need, or cannot afford, to employ men. The big jobs on the farms, such as harvesting and shearing, are let out to the contractors, who have specialized machinery and can finish the jobs in less time. In years gone by, a young lad leaving school could always find work on a farm, although it was often hard and tedious, and the pay was poor, but it was a job, and most of them survived.

Some of the young men around here today work for electricity firms, putting in new poles all over the country — even as far afield as Ireland. This means an early start Monday morning, and often they stay away all week. It is hard, dirty work, but the pay is good. A few men travel to the larger towns and cities to find work, and again, stay away for most of the week. A very few men work from home as builders or carpenters, but this often means that the wife has to go out to work, at least part-time, and while their children are young, the grandmother is often called in to help.

So, all in all, it is still not easy for the local people to live out in these beautiful picturesque places, especially if they have a young family to support. House prices today have gone beyond the reach of our young men, so many of our houses are sold to retired folk who come out from the towns and cities with a healthy bank balance and can enjoy the peace and quiet, and it's good to see them enjoying the countryside.

How different life is today to the life I remember as a child. Sometimes I feel I would like to go back — but not too far! It would be hard without the electricity, the telephone, cars and the good roads. I could go on and on, but I must be thankful I am still here and have good family and friends, who can help me with all this modern technology, which is supposed to make life much easier for everyone.

Yrchen, Yr-ychen or Iyrchyn

I have found all three spellings for this little homestead, but I think originally it would have been called Yr-ychen, which translated from the Welsh means 'the oxen', and this would have been nearer a true meaning of what went on there many years ago.

In the 1891 census, we find a Mrs. Elizabeth Williams aged 60, with her husband James Williams 74, and a son Edward 27, living there. Mrs. Williams was a very proud woman and a very good horsewoman. They had a horse and trap in which they both travelled to Newtown, but it was always Elizabeth at the reins, with James sitting beside her. She would travel very fast, passing the other locals, and with her head held high.

However, by the 1901 census, Jim Williams had died at the age of 84, having spent all his life at Yr-ychen. His father before him had also lived at Yr-ychen, so it had been in the family for a very long time. His father was found dead out on the open hill after a heavy snowstorm.

Elizabeth was now head of the family — was she ever anything else! Living with her were Edward now 37, and Alice, his wife, aged 30, their children Thomas 14, Vera 6, Pryce 5, Gertrude 3 and Charles aged eleven months. Also Fanny aged 2 — a daughter for one of Elizabeth's children. The last five children would have been Edward and Alice's children. James and Elizabeth Williams are both buried in Dolfor Church yard, along with a son who died when he was only 13 years old.

Not so long ago, Iris Reynolds, The Vron, happened to be in Newtown with time on her hands, so she went into the first hairdressing salon she came to and had a 'hair-do'. The lady seeing to Iris started talking and when

Mrs Elizabeth Williams. She must have been a remarkable lady and how smart she looks

she found out that Iris lived in Felindre, said that when she was a child she used to go to her grandmother's for holidays, and granny lived at Yr-ychen. What a good breakthrough, and you need some of these on this job, I can tell you. Iris did not know the name of the salon, but she knew the lady's name. Thank goodness for the telephone, and I eventually got through to the lady. She said that she could not remember much, but her brother, who was older, would remember more. He lived in Kerry and I got in touch with him. One thing he remembered was playing in some strong paddocks. He thought there were six or seven of them, but he had no idea why they were there or why they were so strongly made.

Well, Yr-ychen would give us the answer. This homestead was the nearest place to the Cider House, and the drovers would bring their strongest cattle to pen them in safety overnight, or maybe even longer. These paddocks would most probably have been made even before the Williams family lived there, perhaps even then brigands and wolves roamed the hills, and so these paddocks would keep things out, as well as keep the cattle in.

Now we have a gap in our information. How I wish we were allowed to see the 1911 and 1921 census forms. However, Joan, The Garn, remembers a Bill Swindler living there, and he had been the pig-killer for the Williams family, Yr-ychen. Then Dorothy James remembers a Mrs. Gerrard coming up two or three times a week on Owen's service bus, and bringing some very large dogs on the bus with her. She

Yr-ychen when sold in 2000. It had probably been added to many years ago

Yr-ychen house out across the moor

would take these dogs for long walks on Cilvaesty Hill, and then return to Knighton on the bus. She was a hairdresser in Knighton and Dorothy thought she owned the caravan at Yr-ychen.

When we moved to The Waen in 1956, I remember hearing of a painter living there, and later on an author, but one rough winter, as so often happened back then, and the house would be empty again.

Back in 2000, Iyrchyn — with this spelling — was put on the market with a few acres of land. It was bought by Jane and Mark, originally from Telford. They moved into a quite large caravan in 2002 which they parked up right by the house, and have worked hard, building and repairing the downstairs part of the old house. Then in January 2004, they moved into the house, using the living room as the main bedroom. The rooms upstairs are not safe enough to use yet, but just being in the house is much warmer and more comfortable than in the caravan. Their daughter, Samantha, is attending school in Dolfor, and they also have a little toddler, Natasha — too young as yet for school.

They now have three Welsh mountain ponies — Molly, Thomas and Whisper, and two larger ponies — Snickers and Thomas. They also have two calves, called Bonnie and Bimbo, as pets, and several sheep, so they have really started into the farming world. Jane says she is looking forward to riding round the open hill to collect their sheep, so 'good luck' Jane. It's good to see these very old houses, which have already given a lifetime of warmth and shelter to so many families in the past, used and enjoyed again, and we hope you will all be very happy living at Iyrchyn.

Cider House

This is a large farmhouse just over the brow of the hill on the Knighton / Newtown road. As its name suggests, it was licensed to sell cider since the early days of the drovers and was the last 'resting place' for them before they left Wales and crossed into England and sold the 'stock in their charge' in the English markets.

The cider was made on the premises, the apples being brought there by the 'travelling apple-cart', then put through the cider-press and left to ferment until it was a good strong drink, and very popular with farmers and drovers in those days. I can remember having bottles or flagons of cider out in the hayfield for the men, but as kids we would have a swig when no one was looking! At the Cider House, the cider was sold in the red zinc shed by the road, known as 'The Drovers' Inn'. The shed is still there, but the new owner in 2001 has rebuilt it. It is still zinc, but waiting to be painted — red?

In the 1901 census, we find John Jones 75, as the head, his son John Jones 34, his daughter Sarah Anne 25, and a grandson Charles Jones aged 2, and Jane Thomas 13, a servant. John Jones, senior, lived to be 91, and I have been very fortunate to talk to a grandson of his. This was Jack Davies of Penybank, who also lived to be well over 90. How I wish I had taken notes about the things he told me, but I do remember him telling me about this John Jones, and that he had three other daughters, who would have been out in service in 1901. They were Lizzy, Sally and Cissy, and Cissy was Jack's mother.

Cissy married Stephen Davies, who was the youngest son for John and Mary Davies, Blaen-Nanty, and they started their married life at Blaen-Nanty. They had three boys, Jack, Arthur and Frank, and Jack told me how he loved to visit his grandfather and Uncle John at Cider House. It was still a pub, so men would be calling in for a drink and a chat, especially on a Tuesday on their way home from Newtown market. He remembers his grandfather and a Pryce Thomas often playing dominoes for hours, and probably having a few pints of cider as well. It was a busy and exciting place for children, especially young boys. Also, there would still be a few drovers coming through with their animals. The days of the drovers were just about at an end, and stock lorries and Land Rovers could be seen on the roads, so the few remaining drovers were willing to take geese, pigs and sheep, as well as cattle. What excitement and noise there would be as they came nearer.

Cissy also missed the busy, noisy life at Cider House, and when the Jones family gave up the tenancy, Cissy and her husband desperately wanted to take it on, but her grandfather and the owner of Cider House — a Pugh of Church Stretton — thought that she had enough work looking after her family, and the tenancy was

Cider House farm in the 1990s

given to Mary Anne Wilding, The Ddol, Cwmgwyn, and her husband Fred Davies, Bryn Picca, Mochdre. This was in 1932 and the drovers were no more, so the Davies family spent more time farming. Fred was also the local postman, which in those days was a long walking ticket from Dolfor to Butterwell and across the hill to the Voils, and all places between.

The Davies family had three children — Vincent, Ellis and Edith. Later, Vincent married a Lewis girl from St. Harmon, and went up there to live. Ellis married a local girl, Betty Morgan, and they stayed at Cider House until Ellis retired in 1977, when they moved to Kerry; and Edith married a Pugh from the Clatter area, but has spent many years in nursing homes and, at the moment, is in Newtown. Mary Anne and Fred are both buried in Dolfor Church yard, Fred in 1942 at the age of 50 and Mary Anne in 1958 aged 69. Clarice Mantle, who is a Dolfor girl, was asked to play the organ in the church for Fred's funeral, and she had to enlist the help of her younger sister Freda, who was not really intending to go into the church, but the organ needed wind power, so Freda had to go up to the front to pump the bellows to get power for Clarice to play. This was before the days of foot pedals, and long before electric. Poor Freda was most embarrassed, as she was wearing a bright red coat, and most people wore black or dark colours to a funeral, and definitely not green or red, but she got power to the organ, whatever colour her coat.

When Ellis moved out, Cider House was left empty for a while, and the land was sold. Then, during the 1980s several groups of hippies moved into the house, but one rough winter, and winters are always more stormy and severe up on the top, and Cider House would be empty again.

By the 1990s, the house was in a sorry state of repair, as we can see from the photograph, and we all thought that it would soon be just a heap of rubble, but it was put on the market and a builder bought it.

Cider House today. The large greenhouse is just visible on the left

By the end of the century it was looking good, and the buildings joining the house on both sides were turned into living rooms, making a much bigger house. It was put on the market again at a price which many of us locals thought was extortionate, but it was sold quite quickly. A Mrs. Norman and her son bought it, and although she was quite an elderly lady, but a very fit and active person, wasted no time in wheeling her barrow around, gathering up the builder's rubble, and also jam jars and bottles strewn around by previous tenants. Then she had an enormous greenhouse built and filled it with over four thousand cacti plants of every colour, shape and size. Mrs. Norman invited our Senior Citizens' Club up to see the cacti plants and it was truly a wonderful sight when they were all out in full bloom. She also furnished the interior of the house very lavishly, with no expense spared. What a far cry from the Cider House when it was the Drovers' Inn.

In 2003 Cider House was back on the market with a price tag even higher than before, to enter yet another chapter in its long history.

Today, Cider House has been bought by a Mr. and Mrs. G. Bibbs. They have moved from Preston Capes, a village in Northamptonshire, and although they have only been there a short while, they are enjoying the quiet and the beautiful scenery.

If only walls could talk, what interesting stories would be told.

Cwmgwyn Zion Baptist Chapel

Cwmgwyn Chapel is built very near the source of the River Teme, and was originally built as a Wesleyan Methodist place of worship only half its present size.

The first move to build a place of worship in this area was in 1861, when the Rev. I.E. Page, minister of Kington 1860–1861, wrote a book *A Long Pilgrimage*. The Knighton and district churches were, at that time, in the Kington Wesleyan Methodist circuit. The Rev. Page writes 'Here is a copy of a curious letter sent while I was on the ground of one of our local preachers who had applied for a site for a Chapel.' It was dated June 17th 1861.

Hon Sir,

I take the liberty of sending these few lines to certify that Wm. Marpole of Cwmgwyn and James Davies of Windy Hall begs leave to inform you that since you are wishful to have land in Cwmgwyn to erect a meeting house and school, that the said Wm. Marpole will give you land at the bottom of the hill, and James Davies and Wm. Marpole has together agreed that they will be answerable to the holling of materials that's wanting — stone, sand, lime, timber and slate, and if it your good pleasure to do so, Sir, we are your most obliged and humble servants.

Wm. Marpole and James Davies,
Cwmgwyn, Beguildy.

However, this generous offer was not taken up, which seems to me to be rather a shame, especially after they had written such a good letter. It was sixteen years later when the Rev. Hubert Vavasour Griffiths, a Wesleyan minister who owned The Ddol, gave the ground where the chapel now stands.

We have no records of the actual building of this small Wesleyan chapel, other than it is a stone structure erected in 1877. Several local preachers and class leaders are recorded in the Wesleyan plans — Edwin Griffiths, Devannor; Thomas Griffiths, Cwmgrenglin; R. Griffiths, Coed-y-Hendre; W. Griffiths; J. Price and his brother, T. Price, of Llanbister; Rev. J. James, Cwmgwyn; Rev. J.D. Hamer, Cwmgwyn and the Rev. W.G. Mansfield, Felindre. Were all these Griffiths related to the Rev. H.V. Griffiths, the Ddol? Edwin Griffiths' son married my Auntie Clarice, and they lived at Devannor all their married life and held services in the house. After their days, their children have continued to hold services there for many years, and there would always be tea for everyone in a large upstairs room. Devannor was in the Knighton Methodist circuit, and only closed down in February 2003.

However, the Cwmgwyn Church was never very strong, and in 1886, there were only ten members. Then Edwin Griffiths and J. Price died, T. Price moved down to South Wales, and the Rev. J.D. Hamer, Rev. J. James and the Rev. Mansfield became Baptist ministers. The last record of any activity while still a Wesleyan chapel was Cwmgwyn Sunday School Anniversary, which was held on August 30th 1891, and a tea and public meeting was held the next day.

Around the turn of the century, Mr. Edward Davies and Mr. Abraham Jones moved up from South Wales and both settled in the Cwmgwyn area — Mr. Davies at The Waen and

Mr. Abraham Jones (top) and Mr. Edward Davies

These two families lived as neighbours and are buried side by side

Mr. Jones at Windy Hall. Both these men had earlier left these hilly farming areas and gone down to the coal mines in South Wales, thinking to make their fortune, but they came back to Radnorshire, glad to work in the open air even if the pay was not quite so good.

Both these men were staunch Baptists and, together with the Rev. W.G. Mansfield and Rev. J. James, the Culvert, and other local supporters, they formed a Building Committee. Their aim was to buy the little Wesleyan chapel and extend it and turn it into a Baptist chapel. This sounds quite a straightforward transaction, but according to the deeds, it is anything but, as the following excerpt indicates:

> Know all Men by these Present, that I, John Shaw Banks D.D. President of the Conference of the people called Methodists assembled at Manchester in the County of Lancaster, do hereby testify and declare that the consent of the said Conference is given to the sale of a piece or parcel of land situate lying and being at the Ddol (Cwmgwyn) in the Parish of Beguildy in the County of Radnor, attached to the Wesleyan Methodist Chapel erected on some part or parts thereof, and the said land and Chapel no longer needed for Methodist Trust Purposes.
>
> As Witness my hand this thirteenth day of July One thousand nine hundred and three.
>
> John S. Banks, President

> To the Rev. Thomas Horton, Superintendent Minister of the Knighton Circuit and all others whom it may concern.'

Well there! They are willing to let the Methodist chapel at Cwmgwyn become a Baptist chapel. The actual conveyance of the land is dated 17th December 1903, the transfer being to 'The Rev. William George Mansfield and others'.

It seems that the cost was £5. The men who draw up these deeds should have taken a lesson from Wm. Marpole and James Davies — concise and to the point, but I have heard that they were paid by the number of words they used, so they certainly got their 'pound of flesh'.

Now we must get back to our Building Committee. The Chairman was Rev. W.G. Mansfield; Secretary, J.E. Lewis, Hafod Fadog; Treasurer, Mr. A.L. Jones, Windy Hall, and other members who offered to help in any way — Mr. E. Davies, The Waen; Mr. Pryce Wilding, The Ddol; Mr. J. James, The Garn; Mr. C. Stephens, Cwmgwyn Hall; Mr. S. Davies, Blaen-Nanty; Mr. J. Davies, Bwlch-y-llyn; Mr. R. Morgan, Fiddlers Green; Mr. J. Pugh, Medwaledd; Mr. A. Morris, Brickhouse; Mr. W. Lloyd, High Park and Mr. R. Gwilt, The Cwm, Llanfair Waterdine. The stonemason was Mr. John Bowen, The Mines, Felindre and the carpenter was Mr. John Lewis, The Gravel, Llanbister Road. Most of these men also became trustees of the chapel.

In the very early days of the Baptist chapel, many people joined, and when we look at the members of the Building Committee, if they all came with their family and friends, then the little existing chapel would be full. It was not until 1908 that the extension was built, but the chapel was used by the Baptists even before 1903 when the transfer took place, the Baptists renting it from the Methodists for a couple of years.

For many years it was the centre of all social life in the Cwmgwyn area. Whole families (and families were large in those days) would be coming down from the hills on three sides of the chapel, and those coming up the valley can well remember, in winter-time, the lights from their lanterns bobbing up and down, and making a warm picture on a cold winter's night. Gilbert Pugh, Slate House, remembers his light was a candle in a jam jar. He was a faithful and hard-working member of the chapel for many years and a member of the choir. Even after he moved to Nantmel he would come back to practices and sing in the choir. He also came back on his 90th birthday to the Anniversary — as did Jack Davies, Penybank, and it was good to see them.

In the early days, baptism took place in the River Teme between the chapel and The Ddol. Later, the little brook coming down from Butterwell, passing under the road and joining the Teme below the chapel, was used. Many local people still claim this as being the source of the Teme. This would be dammed or 'stanked up' just above The Culvert house, the little house that was just above where the telephone kiosk is today. One year there were so many candidates that the service was held on two days, and one year, so it is related, the ice on the pool had to be broken first!

Mr. Don Griffiths, the *County Times* photographer about forty years ago, has written to me to tell me about his great-grandfather, Reuben Morgan from Fiddlers Green, an elder of the chapel, dressing up in his best bib and tucker with his tall black hat, and going down to the river dammed ready for a baptism, to check that all was well and, I would think, to pray too. Why he had to dress up so smartly they did not know, but he did so on several days before the baptism. I think he was a very devout Christian, as were many other folk in those early days of the Non-Conformist Revival, and to dress smartly would be out of respect for his Maker.

And here is a report taken from the *Montgomery and Radnor Times* on Tuesday March 28th 1905:

> VELINDRE BAPTISM. — In connection with the Baptist cause at Cwmgwyn on Sunday, the pastor (Rev. W.G. Mansfield) baptized in the River Teme twenty-five persons. On the previous Friday three persons were baptized in the river. The Chapel was crowded on Sunday evening when the pastor received twenty-eight new converts into membership, and two backsliders, and also preached – many being unable to get into the Chapel. Mr. T.D. Hughes, C C. delivered an address in the open air.

Singing has always played a prominent part in the life of Cwmgwyn Chapel and also its Sunday School and the Anniversary. This was always, and still is, held on the last Sunday in June. The well-known and well-loved Mr. A.L. Jones of Windy Hall was Superintendent of the Sunday School for over forty years, and in the early days, Mr. Edward Davies, The Waen, was the conductor. There has always been a good choir with most of the families around producing good singers generation after generation. This was the same with the organists. There was never a shortage, and in those days it would be a pedal organ. Indeed, it has remained a pedal organ right up to the year 2000 when the electric first came to Cwmgwyn and with it an electric organ. Organists whom I have heard of are Mrs. Lilla Wilding, The Ddol; Dorothy Davies, Brickhouse; Mrs. Mills, Medwaledd; Mr. John Stephens, Cwmgwyn Hall;

John Stephens, Joan Lewis, Mrs. Davies of Dolfor and Martin Stephens of Cwmgwyn Hall on their way to have tea in Bwlch-y-llyn Barn to celebrate the Centenary of the Chapel in 1977

Mrs. Laura James, Fiddlers Green; Miss Mary Wilding, Tyn-y-Cwm; Mrs. Margaret Lewis, Criggin and young John Stephens, Cwmgwyn Hall. I can remember when John Stephens (senior) was our main organist Sunday by Sunday, we used to get quite a lot of trouble with the webbing breaking on the one pedal, but that did not bother John. He always seemed to have a nail or a staple handy in his pocket, and the pedal would be working in no time.

With all these very musical families living around Cwmgwyn, and the Sankey hymnbook with its four-part tunes, a good evening of hymn singing would often be enjoyed in the chapel, especially on winters' evenings.

People in those days living up in the hills around Cwmgwyn would often burst into song, and as there were no motorcars, tractors or aeroplanes, they could be heard for many miles around. One local man, namely Johnny Marpole from the Llanarch, remembers when he was young going up the Hendy pitch, ponyback, and listening to George, the Hendy, with his deep bass voice on the one side of the road and Reuben Morgan of Little House, a tenor, on the other side, singing in harmony. If the pitch was a bit too low for George, he'd shout across 'Strike the beggar up a bit, boy.' Reuben duly pitched the hymn up a note and away they'd go again in perfect harmony, while they looked around their sheep and cattle.

There would also be prayer meetings in the week, which would be very well attended. Jack Davies, Penybank, remembers one very windy night when a young lad from up on the hills rushed into the chapel and knelt down to pray — 'O Lord, I do thank thee for not letting this terrible wind blaw [blow] me away.' He must have had a dreadful fright that night. Another prayer which one particular man would pray quite often on stormy weather was 'Oh Lord, please take that terrible black cloud away from the top of Cilfaesty', and yet another prayer, which a farmer in a poor harvest is said to have prayed, 'I do thank Thee Lord for the taters, but oh Lord, they be small this year.'

The Anniversary was a very big day in the life of the little chapel, and still is. It would be packed full of the older folk and young children, but outside the young lads would fill the porch and all around the chapel, tapping at the windows especially if a young girl was singing or reciting on the platform. Mr. Edward Davies would be up the front conducting and in charge of the programme, and Mr. A.L. Jones would be down the back trying to keep control of the boys. One year, it is remembered that Mr. Davies shouted down the back, 'Can you manage them, Mr. Jones?' 'No, boy', came the reply, 'I do believe the Devil is in them tonight', and I do believe he was right because they pulled the whole porch away from the wall, but fortunately no one was hurt. However, these two men struggled for many years trying to keep control of these young lads and I suppose their own lads would be amongst them, and as wicked as any.

Tea would be served between the two services in Friesland House, which is just opposite the chapel. There would be a peat fire, a large fountain full of boiling water, and another fountain full of very hot water on the hob ready to put on to boil. Mr. Bill Watson from Maesyrhelem, who was chairman at our Centenary Services this last

June, told us about the great excitement at the end of the afternoon service. The children would be out through the door, run down the field, jump the river at the bottom and run up the other side trying to be first in for tea. He remembers his mother telling him this, and it would have been over eighty years ago. Bill thought it would have been good if video cameras had been invented by then.

In those days a big round black stove up the front would heat the chapel. Sticks and coal were used, so someone had to light the stove well before the service in wintertime to warm up the chapel, which it would do very well after about an hour. The lighting would be oil lamps — smelly old things until they had been lit a while, but we were all used to them, as that was our means of light at home. Then later Calor gas came on the market and the chapel had gas lighting and heating, and also rings to boil the kettles. The tea was now held in the chapel. I think Mrs. Ella Stephens gave all the gas, lighting and heating and it was still being used right up to the year 2000 when electricity was brought up to the chapel. This is an easier means of lighting and heating, and with no smell of oil or gas.

For many years Cwmgwyn was a thriving little chapel and singing the Sankey hymns had played a big part. I wonder if it would have been such a strong and active chapel had it not been for the Sankey hymnbooks, and here I feel we should give thanks for the many people who wrote the words and composed the tunes, thus making these wonderful four-part hymns.

Ira. D. Sankey was born in Pennsylvania, but both his parents were of English and Irish/Scottish descent. They were both pious Methodists, and both were good singers. They knew how to make a happy home for their nine children, and at the same time bring them up in the fear of the Lord. Young David's first childhood memory was joining the family circle around the log fire, and singing the grand old hymns of the Church — no Sankey hymns in those days!

When talking to some of the folk in the Cwmgwyn area, I have been told almost the same thing. They can remember staying with their grandparents for holidays, and standing around the old pedal organ and singing the Sankey hymns was one of the highlights of their holiday. They remember these days as happy times.

Sankey joined the Methodist Church after leaving school, and his ability for leadership and musical talents were soon recognised. He was elected superintendent of the Sunday School and director of the choir. At this time in America, many churches did not allow the use of an organ or any other musical instrument, regarding these as being worldly and wicked, so Sankey had to depend on the tuning fork to get the pitch for the choir to sing.

Later, the great evangelist Dwight L. Moody heard Sankey singing, and asked if he would join him on his evangelistic campaigns. Moody admitted that he himself had 'no grace in voice or manner'. After quite a few months of soul-searching and deliberating, Sankey agreed and these two men set out on their first tour together around their hometown with Moody preaching and Sankey leading the singing. Everywhere they went the churches, chapels, halls and even the opera houses would be full to overflowing.

Later they both set sail for Liverpool, but they had very little response there at first, as the two men who had invited them to come had both died. They had also been invited to preach in the Y.M.C.A. in York, so there they went. Within a few days there were hundreds crowding into the churches to hear them, and invitations came pouring in from towns and cities in the North, then up into Scotland, and everywhere they went, crowds would gather. It is said that even the shepherds on the hills in Scotland were soon singing the Sankey melodies while tending their sheep. Everywhere Sankey was able to sing his way into the hearts of the people, and was soon acclaimed the most popular sacred singer in Great Britain.

Their tour of Great Britain became long and strenuous, both were tired and they returned to Liverpool ready for their journey home. By this time Liverpool had heard of the two evangelists and several thousands, applauding loudly and singing some of the favourite Sankey hymns, were out on the streets and on the pier to see them leave. And so it was that Moody and Sankey changed the lives of so many people in America, Great Britain and many other parts of the world.

Sankey's very first hymnbook was published in England in 1873, but was only a small pamphlet with just twenty-three songs. He called this first book *Sacred Songs and Solos*. Today our *Sacred Songs and Solos* has 1,200 songs and many of the tunes were composed by Ira D. Sankey.

Cwmgwyn still only uses the Sankey hymnbook, and although many of our books are very old and worn we have found it very difficult to buy new ones. They say they are not being printed any more. In August 1998 we had a very successful Sankey Evening with the chapel really full. Twelve churches and chapels were invited to send in one of their favourite Sankey hymns, and then we made a leaflet containing all the words. Usually as they are favourites, we all know the tunes.

Cwmgwyn is still the only meeting-place in the top end of the valley. Sadly, in 1928 Mr. Edward Davies died at the age of 60. This, indeed, was a great loss to Cwmgwyn but by now, it was a very strong chapel. The work he had helped to start continued on through his children and grandchildren and, of course, the other children and people around. A gentleman from South Wales, whilst up here visiting this area several years ago, remembers singing in a quartet at an eisteddfod in a little chapel some-where around here. He remembered it had a plaque on the wall with the words 'Press on, Brother, Press on' and that is to the memory of Mr. Edward Davies, The Waen, at Cwmgwyn.

Now I am going to include the next story to show the kind of people living in the Cwmgwyn area many years ago. Mr. Doug Jones, Dutlas, remembers coming up to the Cwmgwyn Old Quarry with a troop of fifteen Knighton Boy Cubs. He writes:

> Our transport was a steam traction engine, a Foden road tractor. This wonderful contraption was a shining, hissing, black, gold and brass machine and pulling a huge high-sided trailer, provided by the Radnorshire Coal, Lime and General Supply Co, of Knighton. With parents, families and friends, it looked as if half of Knighton had turned out to see us off.

Tents and cooking gear, supplied by the Territorial Army, were picked up from Machin's barn (now the site of Knighton Library) and a box of bottled pop and bags of sweets, given by B.& J. Davies of Bucknell, were loaded on.

Four motorcars, also solo and combination motorcycles, followed us and we set off, trying to sing above the rattle of our transport, at a healthy eight miles per hour.

On arrival at the quarry, the motorcar people put up the tents, helped by welcoming locals who had cut and stacked more than sufficient bracken for our beds.

At dusk a huge bonfire was lit, then a local group sang to us while we collapsed into our beds.

Next day Miss James, our leader, took us to the source of the River Teme, then a long walk back to a tea-party provided by the local folk and a never-to-be forgotten mini Anniversary-cum-eisteddfod in the Chapel, with local children and parents taking part, as well as some of us.

The next day, being Bank Holiday Monday, we were treated to an impromptu sheepdog trial. Then, we were all packed and loaded, and made our weary way back home. We had had a monumental three-day holiday as guests of the Cwmgwyn people and one we shall never forget.

In 1942, new trustees of the chapel were appointed, as there were only two left from the early days, namely Abraham Jones of Windy Hall, and Reuben Jones of Fiddlers Green. The new trustees were George Pugh, Slate House; John Hamer, High Park; John Stephens, Cwmgwyn Hall; Gilbert Pugh, Slate House; Edward Davies, Brickhouse; John Mills, Little House; John Davies, Gwenlas; Martin Stephens, Hafod Fadog; John Easson Davies, Bwlch-y-llyn; Burton Stephens, Cwmgwyn Hall; William Pryce Pugh, Slate House and David Thomas Pugh, Slate House.

During the next decade the numbers at the chapel fell dramatically. The Davies family, The Waen, and the Jones family of Windy Hall had mostly moved or passed away, the little houses on the hills were left empty and the numbers attending Cwmgwyn were steadily getting less each year. When Doug and I moved into The Waen in 1956 the numbers on the stage on the Anniversary were very low. Doug and I both joined the choir right away and Doug sang duets with Ruby Davies, who had moved from The Waen to Newtown, and was also in quartets. Doug was a good singer.

John Stephens, Cwmgwyn Hall, was the leader of the chapel by this time, and Mrs. Mills, Medwaledd, was the organist. I joined the chapel quite soon as I was already a Baptist. Doug, although Church, would come to Chapel sometimes and, of course, always when Anniversary time was getting near. John Stephens also had a concert party and we would go round singing in small chapels and village halls, usually trying to raise money for the little chapel to keep going. We had a lot of fun on these little outings.

Then in 1975 John married Margaret Savage from Llanfair Caereinion, and they soon had their three children. This gave great hope to the few members left

A wedding present to Margaret and John, 1975.
Back row (left to right): Jim James, Martin Stephens, Albert Price, Gilbert Pugh. Middle row: Doug Thomas, Alma Davies, Margaret Huffer, Blodwyn Brick, Clarice Thomas, Tilda Price, Glen Davies, Koreen Davies, Mrs. L.M. Richards, Rene Lewis, Margaret Lewis, Margaret and John, John Davies, Mrs. Ruby Davies, Rev. L.M. Richards

in Cwmgwyn, and they have certainly helped to keep the doors open Sunday by Sunday ever since.

The three Stephens children have sung and recited at the Anniversaries since they were very small as, of course, have most of the other children living around. Our six children have all taken part at Cwmgwyn at least until they went to Grammar School. During the last few years of John's life and when his children were up in their teens, the whole family, Margaret, John, and the three children, would sing quintets, which were very popular and gave a lot of pleasure at Cwmgwyn and also at other chapels around.

As long as I remember, John has been in charge of running the chapel. He was chairman, secretary, treasurer, choir-master and organist — indeed, John *was* Cwmgwyn, and when sadly he died in February 1997 at the age of 76, we were all like lost sheep.

In the following Spring we had several meetings to try to decide whether to keep the chapel open or close it down. We were only about twelve members left, and all of us nearing the 70-mark — if not older. Since then we have lost Mrs. Joyce Evans, Mrs. Koreen Davies, Mr. and Mrs. Mills and two of their sons, and Mr. and Mrs. Arthur Brick.

Some years before, Bryan and Gwyneth McCann had retired and moved back to Lower Fiddlers Green. Gwyneth is the granddaughter for the late Mr. Edward Davies, The Waen, and she was soon back on the stage singing as she had done many years before, and Bryan also joined the choir.

Then in August 1997 Gwyneth and Bryan joined the chapel, both having been baptized in Llanidloes a few weeks before. This was good news for us. We also had David and Frances Morris who had moved to Pound Gate, join us, and they were both good singers and soon in the choir. Then last year Wendy and David Lambourne from Cwm House joined us and they are regular attendees at the services and both in the choir. So any talk about closing down the chapel were forgotten, although we still had a lot of work to do.

We knew nothing about the records or the deeds of the chapel, so we invited Mr. Meredith-Powell, secretary of the Baptist Union of Radnor and Montgomery, to help us. Firstly, we discovered that we only had one trustee left out of the fourteen in 1942, and that was Mr. Gilbert Pugh who by now was living in Nantmel and was well over 80 years old. Seven new trustees were invited to join, some from other Baptist chapels in the area. Mr. Philip Vallance Q.C. who has Little House as his holiday home, offered to witness the signing in of the new trustees, and Rev. John Bridge acted as chairman. The seven new members were Mr. Clifford James, Cwmgwyn; Mr. Arthur Brick, Cwmgwyn; Mr. William Manuel, Bwlchsarnau; Mr. William Watson, Maesyrhelem; Mr. Walter Evans, Knucklas; Mr. George Wilding,

Blod and Arthur had this little bungalow built in 1978 and lived there happily until Arthur died in 2000 and Blodwyn in 2001. They always kept a good garden with beautiful flowers. Both are buried in Felindre Baptist chapelyard

Cwmgwyn; and Mr. Bryan McCann, Cwmgwyn.

Next, we only had one deacon, namely our faithful Clifford James. Mrs. Blodwyn Brick who had been Sunday School treasurer for many years and myself, Clarice Thomas, were appointed. The new committee was formed with Bryan as chairman, Gwyneth treasurer, myself secretary and Blodwyn Brick as Sunday School treasurer.

The chapel was in need of repairs, so we applied for several grants, but to no avail. It was then agreed that we do the work ourselves as much as we could, then try to have more functions at the chapel to help increase our bank balance. Bryan suggested a 'Sankey Evening', which, with a rush, we managed to get organised for the 17th August 1997. This was very enjoyable and very successful and over £200 was raised.

Dianne and Robert's wedding day with her godparents Blodwyn and Arthur Brick and her cousin Heather Griffiths

We now had an offer from the Electricity Board to connect the chapel, which we could not turn down. We had applied years before but the amount then was well over our bank balance. This new offer was well within our limit, so the electric was brought up to a box outside the chapel until the inside had been repaired.

Bryan had drawn up plans for the work to be done, and we were all happy with them. So with Bryan as boss, work commenced. The two brothers, Christopher and Brian Roberts, The Forge, were asked to move the soil at the back with their tractors and digger. Then for some of the heavy work like replacing the joists for the new floor and putting the new floor down, Bryan asked for help from some of the chapel supporters. These strong men were John Stephens, David Morris, George Wilding and his two sons.

The floor was done in stages as our ordinary Sunday services continued. At one time when the front part of the floor was missing, Bryan put two planks down for access to the pulpit. Mr. Ray Lloyd of Knighton was our preacher for that Sunday and he now boasts that he had to 'walk the plank' in order to deliver his sermon.

Bryan had organised new windows and doors to be put in. There was also the heating and lighting to be installed. He and Gwyneth were there to supervise the firms doing the work.

Then they both set to work. They worked hard for days, and weeks, and months, plastering and making good the walls, then painting the ceiling and walls, carpeting the floor wall to wall and even using the spare carpet on the seats for extra comfort!

Every time we had a service, we were all truly amazed at the improvements that had taken place — and by two retired people. We did offer to help, but I think they were happy doing it on their own. Your grandfather, Gwyneth, would have been very proud of you both if he could see Cwmgwyn Chapel now — the little chapel he worked so hard to get started nearly one hundred years ago.

When most of the work had been finished and the chapel looked good, we had a wonderful surprise. John Stephens and Mair Thomas (Frances Morris's daughter) asked if they could be married in Cwmgwyn Chapel. I felt that this was a wonderful 'thank you' to Bryan and Gwyneth and their helpers for all their hard work.

Of course, we have never had a licence for weddings in Cwmgwyn before, but Bryan sorted that out and the wedding took place on a beautiful day in May 2001. What an ending to nearly one hundred years as a Baptist chapel.

Putting down the new floor

The very first wedding in Cwmgwyn chapel : Mair Thomas and John Stephens were married in May 2001

The Friends of the chapel presented Mair and John with a Black Forest cuckoo clock, and when it was presented, the choir and the children sang the Cuckoo Song. Later in the year Alwena Stephens and Charles Campbell were married in Felindre Chapel, and the Friends of the chapel presented this couple with a painting of the Prysg as it stood before the renovations had started.

Bryan and his helpers are now busy making a small tearoom at the back of the chapel, and also toilets. Both these facilities are desperately needed, and we hoped it would all be finished before our centenary celebrations in 2003.

In 2004 the tearoom and toilets were finished and in use at our centenary services, and what an improvement on the many years before when we have struggled to make the tea in the back of the chapel, which was usually full of people.

Here is the report in our local paper, sent in by Mr. John Peregrine, who over many years has been a loyal supporter, and very good friend, of the little chapel:

Delighted congregation marks 100 years of Christian worship

For over 140 years, Christian worship has taken place at a remote building at the top of the Teme Valley, close to the source of the River Teme.

In 1861 negotiations took place to purchase land to build a Wesleyan Methodist Chapel at Cwmgwyn.

In July 1903, Edward Davies of The Waen Farm, together with his good friends and neighbours Abraham Jones of Windy Hall, Reuben Morgan of Fiddlers Green, the Rev. W.G Mansfield of Felindre, and many supporters, bought the Wesleyan chapel and it became Zion Baptist Chapel, which it remains to this day though most locals know it as Cwmgwyn.

At a recent celebratory service, when the chapel was absolutely full, Mr. William Manuel extended greetings and congratulations to members from the Radnorshire and Montgomeryshire Baptist Association and reminded those present of these facts.

For the Centenary Service, Mrs. Clarice Thomas welcomed everyone and introduced the President, Mr. Bill Watson of Llanbadarn Fynydd, who explained to the congregation that many of those taking part in the service were relatives of the original founders of the chapel. ...

In his address, Mr. Watson said how delighted he was to see the chapel full and so many children as well as adults participating in the service. He also stressed how we must move with the times, being less concerned about our dress for attending places of worship and more concerned with making our services attractive to young people.

In many churches, we seem to be set in the past, unwilling to make changes. We have to find ways of encouraging young people to attend regularly and take part in the services, becoming involved in running our places of worship.

What was happening in Cwmgwyn at this service was a shining example of what could be done, he said, getting youngsters as well as the more established members to take part. ...

Time waits for no man, and so we move on. But I feel I must thank everyone who came and supported us in many different ways on that day, especially those who came back as our special guests to give continuity to our worship, and also all who came to listen and to help with the tea and, above all, to talk and catch up with news of friends and families of yesteryear. It was good to join together in thanksgiving for our little chapel on the hillside and to remember with love and gratitude all the many, past and present, who gave so much of their time and talents to make and keep it the special place it is today.

A very full chapel for the Anniversary service in 1998. Look at the stools and benches coming in at the back

A platform full of children and little Arthur being held up on the right watching Keith on his guitar. Anniversary service, 1998

Margaret Lewis, Joan Lewis and Keith Thomas

Part of our little choir preparing to sing. From left to right: Bryan McCann, Joan Lewis, Wendy Lambourne, John Stephens (largely hidden), Gwyneth McCann, Meg Savage, David Morris, Frances Morris and David Lambourne . We are all getting older, and take longer to get ready!!

Nativity Plays
Left and above: The Angels, Shepherds and Mary & Joseph
Lower left: The Shepherds in 2003: Ben Harris, Robert Hart, George Morgan, Jo Barnett and Seb Barnett
Below: Christmas 2000

Little Corrie Meredith joins the children on stage

Christmas 2002
Back row (from left to right): Ruth Corbett, Eva Corbett, Frances Williams, Jess Barrett, Hannah Meredith, Thomas Corbett, Kim Barnett, Ieuan Thomas
Middle row: Tom Harris, Grace Corbett, Jamie Thomas, Charlie Reynolds, Gethyn Thomas
Front row: Gareth Watkins, Kate Reynolds, Ben Harris

Cwmgwyn trip to the sea-side, 1999

Dorothy James having a laugh with Bill the Garn and Bill the Rhuvid

Sidney Meredith, Richard George and Bert Williams

From left to right: Jack Barrett, George Thomas, Lily Thomas, Jessica Barrett, More Thomas and Ieuan Thomas. Annette Thomas's little boy shouted 'fetch a kettle of hot water mum, it's freezing'

A seagull has wished Helen Barrett 'good luck' on her shoulder, whilst Jayne Harris is glad to be out of the firing line

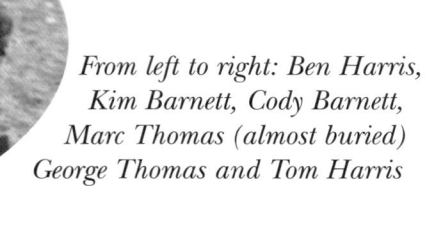

From left to right: Ben Harris, Kim Barnett, Cody Barnett, Marc Thomas (almost buried) George Thomas and Tom Harris

Christmas 1999 at Cwmgwyn Chapel. All the children, with a parent helping, lit a candle at the back of the chapel and carried it up to the front. The parent put the candle in the 2000 holder which Bryan had made. We all sang:
One More step along the world I go
From the old year to the new
Keep me travelling along with you.

The Ddol Farm, Cwmgwyn

This dwelling started its life as a little clod house or *ty-un-nos*, and would have had a small patch of hill ground around it. It was originally called Cwmgwyn Cottage.

We do not really know when a lot of these little homesteads were built, but I think they were an ongoing feature through the 18th and 19th centuries and even into the very early part of the 20th century, until the Earl of Birkenhead's change in the law in 1905.

I have also been told that the road or track, suitable for walkers and pony transport, came down off the open hill, through The Ddol fold and on down past where the chapel is today. Then it followed the river in the valley, passing quite near to The Gravel and Hafod Fadog and up to the road where it is today, joining near Cwmgwyn Hall.

In the 1891 census the property is known as The Ddol, which means 'house in the meadow', and the family living there were the Wildings, who are still living

The Wilding family, The Ddol.
Above, from left to right: Pryce Stephen, Mary Anne,
Mr. Pryce Wilding holding Bert, Una, Ella, Mrs. Mary Wilding
with Dora on her knee and Eveleyn.
Left: Dora a few years later!

there today. Mr. Pryce Wilding 45, a farmer; his wife Mary 29, who was a daughter for the Stephens, Cwmgwyn Hall; Rachael Stephens 70, mother-in-law; Una 7, daughter; Pryce Stephen 3; Mary Anne 2; and Evelyn, nine months old, lived there; also Mary Jones 17, a domestic servant, and Edward Davies 22, a servant. (Might he have been the Edward Davies, The Waen, before he married and went down to South Wales?) By the time of the 1901 census, Ella 8, daughter; Bert 5, son; Dora 2, and John 1, had all been added to the family.

The Wilding families have lived at The Ddol for over a hundred and thirty years, so they must have been there before Cwmgwyn Chapel was built. The property was owned by the Rev. Hubert V. Griffiths, and he also owned Tyn-y-Cwm. (One of our very senior citizens, who have now died, used to say that Mrs. Griffiths, who lived at The Gravel, was

From left to right: John Reynolds (Rhyd-y-Cwm), Frank Davies (Dafern), John Wilding, Lilla Davies, John Davies (Gwenlas) and Ruth Reynolds (Rhyd-y-Cwm). John Wilding married Lilla Davies

the mother of these two Griffiths boys.) It was not until 1983 that George bought The Ddol.

Una, The Ddol, married Charles Stephens of Cwmgwyn Hall, and they started their married life at the Hall. Mary Anne married Fred Davies, Brynpicca, Mochdre, and they moved into the Cider House in 1932, but its days as a busy drovers' 'resting place' had just about come to an end by then. Evelyn moved to South Wales, but I don't think he was ever married. Pryce Stephen married Elizabeth Reynolds from Pencwm, Llaithddu, and they moved to Tyn-y-Cwm with Bert, a younger brother, who also never married. Elizabeth had three daughters — Iris, Joan and Mary — but, sadly, Elizabeth was never a strong woman and died while the girls were still quite young. All three girls have always supported Cwmgwyn, and Mary, who was a very good organist, used to come and play the organ while John Stephens would conduct the choir on Anniversary days.

Several years later Ella married John Stephens and they moved into Cwmgwyn Hall with Una and Charles, so two sisters and two brothers lived at the Hall for a few years. Then Una and Charles moved to Hafod Fadog with their two youngest children, Olwen and Martin, but Burton stayed on at the Hall. Dora married William Reynolds and they lived at The Walk Mill. Their children were Anne — who married David George — Billy and Eric.

John Wilding, the youngest child, who was still living at The Ddol, married Lilla Davies, a daughter from The Waen, and they continued to live at The Ddol. Lilla was the main organist at the chapel for many years. They had two sons, Ronald and George. Ronald joined the Navy and later lived in Newtown, and George married Marcia McCann, a daughter for Bryan and Gwyneth. George and Marcia also have two sons — John and Gwynfor, and they all live at The Ddol. George is now a trustee of the chapel, and all the family have helped in the recent repairs and improvements that have taken place at the chapel since the year 2000.

And so The Ddol and its owners and occupants have always been involved in the building and supporting the little chapel of Cwmgwyn, which is on their doorstep.

Walk Mill

This little cottage has just been sold in 2005. The woollen mill has long gone and is nearly forgotten, and the house will need a lot of money, work and TLC to get it back to a liveable home.

Walk Mill in 2004 when Eric and Joan came to Wales for a holiday. Eric, Iris, Billy and his wife Molly are standing outside, whilst Joan took the photograph. Iris was the owner of the property and is a cousin to these two boys

The first couple we hear about living there are Alice and Jim Williams and their son Richard. They then moved to the Nest and Dora and William Reynolds moved into Walk Mill with their three children: Eric, Anne and William (Billy). This family had been living at Killowent. Dora was the youngest daughter of the Wilding family, the Ddol, and William was a son for the Reynolds family of Rhyd-y-Cwm.

Eric is married to Joan and they live in Australia. They have a daughter Selena who is a schoolteacher in Melbourne. Anne married David George, The Moat, and they lived at Cefn Derw. They have three children: Wyndham, Richard and Kate. Sadly Anne died several years ago. Billy married Molly and they have three sons: Peter John, Andrew and Mark.

Dolfrynog

This is a very small cottage, and most probably one of our little *ty-un-nos* homesteads, and is just along the lane from Cwmgwyn Chapel.

In the 1901 census, a James Davies 92, Elizabeth 69 his wife, John a son, and two grandchildren, Maurice and George, lived there. I have heard from Ruth Morgan, Dolyfelyn, who is a great-great-granddaughter for Elizabeth and James, who told me that her grandparents were Rose — a daughter from Yrchyn — and Maurice. This couple had eleven children, so with parents and grandparents living in that little house, there must have been times when it was very full. In those days, many a home kept their grandparents with them. The alternative was the workhouse.

The children attended Crug-y-Byddar School and Cwmgwyn Chapel. Ruth says that granny made all the children's clothes, baked bread most days, as well as helping out on the farm. Also, she would walk to Newtown once a week to get groceries for the family. Later, they had a pony and trap, which must have made life a little easier. The children used to go up on the hill during school holidays to pick whimberries, which were quite plentiful in those days. They were a cheap source of money, and with not nearly as many sheep kept on the open hills as there are today, the children could pick enough for granny to take to Newtown to sell. She would then buy new boots in which the children would go back to school. Rose died in 1947 aged 71, and Maurice died in 1959 aged 81. Both are buried in Dolfor Church yard.

Ruth's mother, Bessie, came to work for the Wildings, The Ddol, and was nanny to Ronald and George. She met Fred, one of the eleven children, and they were married and first went to live at Butterwell. Later, I hear, they moved to Upper Green, Llanbadarn, and then they moved to

Maurice Davies at his daughter's wedding in 1920

Cwmcorn in Dolfor. They had four children — Ruth, Margaret, Dennis and Bill, who was always referred to as 'Bill Cwmcorn'. He was a good footballer in his younger days.

Fred had trained as a wheelwright and carpenter, which would have been very useful crafts in those days. Fred and Bessie kept faithful to Cwmgwyn Chapel, and Bessie became very good friends with Blodwyn Brick, who was our Sunday School treasurer and a deacon of the chapel.

Crug-y-Byddar School around 1927
From left to right. Back row: Ralph Williams (Lane House), Frank Jones (The Oaks), Jack Davies (Dolfrynog), Martin Stephens (Cwmgwyn Hall), Mr. Ward (Headmaster), Mrs. Ward (Teacher), George Davies (Dolfrynog), Hubert Reynolds (Rhyd-y-Cwm), William Marpole (Green Hollow), Dick Marpole (Hill Top).
Second row: Olwen Stephens (Cwmgwyn Hall), May Lakelin (Cefn-Bedw), Lily Pugh (Slate House), Mildred Hamer (High Park), Aggie Stephens (Hendy), Patty Owens (Shell Heath), Florie Price (The Square), Mary Stephens (Cwmgwyn Hall), Grace Williams (Lane House), May Hamer (High Park), Patty Williams (New House), Jenny Williams (New House).
Third Row: Vida Williams (New House), Jessie Smith (The Culvert), Beattie James (Fiddlers Green), Mary Marpole (Hill Top), Tilda Jones (Windy Hall), Frances Marpole (Green Hollow), Louise Reynolds (The Vron), Edith Pugh (The Turgey), Mary Marpole (Gate House), Dorothy Davies (Brick House), Joan Ward (School House), Freda Ward (School House), Edith Reynolds (Vron).
Front row: John Marpole (Green Hollow), Jack Williams (New House), Mal Brick (The Forge), Lesley Brick (The Forge), Arthur Pugh (Turgey), Fred Jones (The Oaks), Henry Pugh (Tynllwyn), John Stephens (Cwmgwyn Hall), Jim James (Fiddlers Green), Ken Jones (The Stores), Ellis Davies (Cider House), Harry Williams (Lane House), Frank Marpole (Llanerch), Cliford Pugh (Dutlas)

In the very hot weather Mr. Ward would dam the river Teme near the school and the children would have a swimming lesson. The children would also be out gardening for the boys, and weaving or sewing for the girls

George was the son who stayed at home and farmed there. He was also the local postman, as we hear from Mr. Walter Bufton, who worked at The Llethrau in 1932. George married Lily Evans from Cwmadolfa. They had four children born at Dolfrynog, then they moved to Tregynon. Their children were Vaunda, Olwen, Joyce and Norman.

I have not heard much about the children of the other nine out of the eleven, except that just recently Joyce, one of George's children, has sent me some information about Crug-y-Byddar School. Mr. and Mrs. Ward were the teachers and Joyce has seen the log book and the punishment book. She says her dad, George, and his brothers Fred, Jack and Horace are mentioned for such things as swearing, playing in the churchyard and cutting their desks, for which they received 'strokes across the desk'. Sounds a bit painful!

The next family to live at Dolfrynog were Mr. Tom James and his wife Laura Jane, who used to live at Fiddlers Green. This family were all faithful to Cwmgwyn Chapel. Laura Jane was a descendant of Naomi and Richard Morgan, and was very talented in both singing and playing the organ. She died in 1956 aged 67, and Tom died in 1959 aged 69. This couple were the last of the local 'old folk' to live there.

Lilian and George Davies's children: Norman (at the back), Vaunda, Olwen and Joyce

Dolfrynog in 1966

The Maypole Dance was revived at Beguildy school in the 1970s. Doug and Colin Edwards made the pole, and I remembered the dance from my school days. When Crug-y-Byddar school closed in 1955 all the children had to go to Beguildy School

The Rev. M. Wishart leaves Beguildy. In this picture are the Headmaster John Peregrine and Michael Wishart, the school staff and governors and over 70 children. This would be sometime between 1980 and 1984

Some time later I think it was sold to an Australian, Colin Edwards, who had settled with his wife and family at the Lane House. He put a new roof on Dolfrynog and did some other repairs, then he sold it to Mr. and Mrs. Ron Pritchard. Ron worked in the engineering industry in the Midlands, and would come out most weekends and holidays and, with his stonemason, work hard repairing and rebuilding until, from the front, it looked more like a mansion than a little *ty-un-nos*, but he has kept the original shape and size of the old house at the back. He has also made a very large fishpond with the River Teme as its supply of fresh water.

In 2003, when Mair Thomas and John Stephens were married in Cwmgwyn Chapel, which is very close to Dolfrynog, they had their photographs taken down by the pool — an ideal setting for a wedding photograph.

Mr. and Mrs. Pritchard are keen fishermen, and spend a lot of time in different parts of the country on fishing holidays, but they also come back to Dolfrynog and enjoy their holiday home.

The Culvert

This is another of our little houses built in one night. It was situated just above where the Cwmgwyn telephone kiosk is today — but maybe not for much longer. The 'powers that be' are threatening to remove all these kiosks out in the isolated hilly areas — which I would think is the very place they are most needed, especially as our new mobile phones do not work around here. We do seem to have some 'right 'uns' in our offices today. Common sense seems to be a thing of the past!

The first person we hear about living at The Culvert was the Rev. J. James, who earlier had emigrated to Canada, but returned to these parts. He was a Methodist

*In a Sunday School trip to the sea-side.
From left to right. Back row:
Ivor Jones (Jack, Windy Hall's son), Cliff James.
The four ladies: Mrs. Lloyd (The Culvert), Mrs. James (Cliff's mum), Lily Pugh (Slate House), Mrs. Pugh (Slate House).
The children: Sybil Lloyd (The Culvert), Trevor Jones (Windy Hall), Iris Lloyd (The Culvert), Kitty James (Fiddlers Green)*

minister, and together with the Rev. H.V. Griffiths, who owned The Ddol Farm, was involved in the building of the Wesleyan chapel at Cwmgwyn in 1877.

Then in the 1891 census, William Crewe 82, his wife Elizabeth 75, and their daughter Mary 38, lived there with Mary's children George and David, twins aged 5, and Oliver, three months old. Also, there were three N.C. children, as they were recorded in the census — Cissy Jones 3, John Price 1, and Frank Owens, six months old. N.C. stood for Nursing Children, who for some reason could not be brought up by their parents, and a small amount of money would be given to the family looking after them to help with the housekeeping. With nine people in this small house — two quite old and six young children — I would think that poor Mary needed it.

I have also heard that a Don Crewe's son was in Mochdre School with Joan, The Garn, and he married a sister to Tom, The Smithy at Dolfor. Also, Tudor of the 'Tudor and Corfield' electrical firm in Newtown married a daughter from The Culvert.

By 1901 Mary was the head of the household, so the two parents had probably died. Mary still had her son Oliver, now 10 years old, and three boarders — or as they used to be called N.C.s — John Price 11, Frank Owens 10 and Suzanne Morgan 2. Her twin boys, now 15 years old, were working at Bwlch-y-llyn.

Mary died in 1914 at the age of 60. She is buried in the old yard at Felindre, and on her headstone is the following verse:

> Farewell my friends and children dear
> For you I have toiled for many a year
> I have always strove to do my best
> And now I have gone to take my rest

I think poor Mary had well earned her rest.

Later we hear of George Lloyd, a son for Polly Lloyd, who lived in the middle house at Lane House. George worked at the Hendre and advertised for a housekeeper. A Lillian Smith came up from South Wales with her two children, Ivor and Jessie Smith. Some time later Lillian and George were married and moved to The Culvert. While there, they had five children — Sybil, Iris, Edward, Bernard and Graham.

I have recently heard from Edward, who now lives in Bayston Hill with his wife Pamela, whom I taught in school. He can remember a few things about The Culvert, although they moved when he was about six years old.

He remembers Kitty James, Fiddlers Green being baptised in the river just above The Culvert, and she came into this house to get dry and change her clothes. Cliff James of Fiddlers Green was also a good friend of the Lloyd family, as indeed were most neighbours, especially in the less wealthy areas up around Cwmgwyn. What they lost out in money, they made up for in kindness and helpfulness to one another, and many of the families were in the same financial state.

Edward Lloyd and Cliff James at Gerald and Dorothy's party

Crug-y-Byddar School. Clockwise: Miss Reese (Teacher), Mary Wilding, Vaunda Brick, Trevor Jones, Cliff James, Lesley Webster, John Roberts, Bert Goodman, Clifford Marpole, Ray Jones, Emrys Lewis, Olwen Williams. In the middle is Joyce Davies and an unidentified child

Edward also remembers in the late 1930s a severe storm. The culvert under the bridge was blocked and, as a result, the house was flooded to about four to five feet of muddy water.

The children from The Culvert would have gone to Crug-y-Byddar School and Cwmgwyn Chapel. Of course, it was only walking, or maybe a bike if you were lucky.

Dorothy, Brickhouse, and her husband, Gerald Scott have just had a big celebration — I think sixty years of happy married life together — and Edward and his wife attended and met up with several Cwmgwyn people, including Cliff and Margaret and Edward, The Criggin. They all had a good old chat about years gone by, which in many childhood memories were very happy days.

I have heard that George served in both World Wars and came home safely from both. In later life, he would write articles on health and aids to healthy living.

Both Lillian and George are buried in the new yard in Felindre, and I can hear of no one else living at The Culvert. When we moved to The Waen in 1956, the house was still standing and seemed in fair condition, but there is no trace of it today.

Bwlch-y-llyn

The first family we hear about living at Bwlch-y-llyn were the Hamers. Mrs. Dorothy Manuel, Blaen-y-cwm, Llanbister was one of this Hamer family before she married Billy Manuel, who incidentally, is a trustee of Cwmgwyn Chapel, so yet another connection with this area. They invited me over to see the family tree, which she had researched, and which goes back to the 18th century. What an interesting afternoon I spent with them.

It seems that an Abraham Hamer married Anne Wozencraft, from Rhyd-moel-ddu, Llananno, and came to live at Bwlch-y-llyn. Their first son was born in 1805 and was also named Abraham. It seems that in years gone by, most first sons and daughters had the same name as their parents. They did not have much post in those days and no telephone directories to look through, so I suppose it didn't matter so much as today.

This second Abraham Hamer married Mary Evans from Gwary-car, Llananno, and in 1830, this couple were still living at Bwlch-y-llyn. There was also a Henry Hamer living at Rhyddir Oak, with his nephews John and Neville Hamer, and also several Hamers around Beguildy.

I have included these Hamer families because many of you have read in the *Mid-Wales Journal* in the summer of 2004 about the trouble caused when the Beguildy Church people removed some railings from a rather large grave, because the railings had become unsafe. Well, the five people buried in those graves were the same Hamers as those living at Bwlch-y-llyn. The Hamers who used to live at Trebrodier are also on that family tree.

One Hamer, now living in America, has been in touch with Richard Brock of Brandy House and wonders if he was the same Richard Brock who was at school in

Worcester with his sons. Richard then passed on this letter to me and I wrote to this family in Dakota, America, and sent over a copy of all that was written on the five graves. He says that his daughter is going to come over with him this summer to look up the places where their family used to live, and also to meet Mrs. Dorothy Manuel and look at this wonderful family tree. It makes all this work of researching and writing the history of our area seem worthwhile, especially if they have travelled great distances and can take photographs of maybe a house, a church or even a headstone back with them.

In the 1891 census Bwlch-y-llyn was empty, but by 1901, a John Lewis and his wife Jane were living there, and George and David Crewe, the twin boys aged 17 from The Culvert, both worked at the property.

The next family we hear about were the Davieses. A young servant girl, Jane Easson, had come down from Scotland with the Haig whisky people. They had bought Penithon Hall in the Llaithddu and also several farms on the Penithon estate. Jane worked at the Hall for several years, then met and married John Davies who was living at Bwlch-y-llyn. They had one son, John Easson, but John the father was much older that Jane, and not in very good health. He died in 1935 at the age of 72. Young John and his mother carried on farming for many years. Jane was as strong as any man and could do most jobs on the farm. They were still living in the small cottage, which by its size I would think would be one of our *ty-un-nos* houses.

When we first moved to the Waen in 1956, I used to go down to Bwlch-y-llyn once a week to collect our four loaves of bread and a few groceries, which I think J.O. Davies of Llandrindod would have brought out to Bwlch-y-llyn. I would take my big pram with one, two or three boys in, and after a talk with Mrs. Davies, would load the bread and groceries into the well of the pram, put the shelf back in, then the boys, and walk back to the Waen. Sometimes, Mr. Hamer of High Park would be there with his pony and small cart to collect his bread and sometimes a sack of corn or other foodstuff for his animals. Mr. James of Dolfrynog would also come with his sack to collect his bread.

John Easson married Koreen Morris, whose grandparents used to live at Brickhouse. Mr. A. Morris was on the Building Committee of Cwmgwyn Chapel. Koreen was a war widow, having first married Garfield Rees of Presteigne, who was killed on active service at the end of the war.

Koreen and John Easson Davies

The new house at Bwlch-y-llyn

Both Koreen and John were faithful members of Cwmgwyn Chapel and both sang in the choir. At one time, they gave a very generous donation to the chapel, which was used to build the high retaining wall outside, thus making the road quite a lot wider, so allowing more cars to park. They also gave the oak gate at the entrance to the chapel ground, which is still there.

Koreen and John had a little son in the early 1960s but, very sadly, he died at birth, and is buried with his grandparents. Later, they built a new house further back from the road, but they left the little old house as it was, and it is still there. I think this is a good example of a *ty-un-nos* house.

Jane died in 1974 in her 98th year and is buried with her husband in Felindre. She had been a remarkable lady. I have often seen her outside chopping sticks, and she could swing that axe as high as any man.

John was secretary of the Felindre Sports Committee for many years when it was one of the biggest Sports anywhere around. There would be horse racing, with several bookies on the field, motor-bike racing, as well as all the usual running and jumping competitions and, of course, foot-

Mrs. Jane Davies

ball matches going on until it was just about too dark to see the ball. This must have taken a lot of organising, and the committee members had their work cut out to get it all running smoothly and on time.

John died in 1979 at the age of 72 and is buried in Felindre. Koreen then sold the property and first moved to Crossgates where she lived for several years. Then she went into a home in Llandrindod and later died in 2001 at the age of 83, and is buried in Felindre with her husband.

The next couple to live at Bwlch-y-llyn are Dorothy and Michael Chatterley, originally from Lancashire. This couple soon got into the spirit of the countryside and all kinds of animals could be seen out in the fields around Bwlch-y-llyn — sheep of several different colours and kinds, cattle, pigs and all different kinds of poultry, including peacocks — well! We had never seen the like of it in the Cwmgwyn area before! Indeed, we would often refer to them as Mr and Mrs. Noah, or sometimes Dr. Dolittle, but they took it all in good part. Sadly, in 2001, when foot and mouth broke out at the Waen, all the stock at Bwlch-y-llyn were slaughtered. It was a sad and cruel time, but we lived through it.

When I started researching for this book, Dorothy came with me to Llandrindod library to copy out — by hand — the 1891 census forms, so she has been involved in the writing of the history of our area. Michael has been doing repairs on the old house, trying to keep it much as it looked over a hundred years ago. He has also started farming again and has bought two sheep.

The Waen

To write a history of the Waen, I must go back to the 1820s when Edward Parker lived there in the 'old house'. This was across the top of the meadow and just up in the well field. In those days, homes were built near a spring or at least near running water — a good idea too, as I found out to my cost when we moved to the Waen, many, many years later.

In 2000 our Womens' Institute decided to survey all the graveyards in the area. One afternoon, I had been in the old yard in Felindre Baptist, trying to record all the names on the headstones. What a job! As some were overgrown with moss and ivy, it was very difficult to read all that was written, and in those days most headstones had a verse or a portion of Scripture as well as names and dated. A bowl of soapy water and a scrubbing brush were needed on some of these stones, and one day I had had a hard battle with one particular stone, but I had stuck to until at least I had the names and ages of the people buried there.

I came home quite late and rather exhausted. But as I sat down hoping for a well-earned rest, in walked Bono Barrett, very excited. He told me that an American lady had stopped him out on the road, and asked him for information about people living around here many years ago. 'Follow me!' said Bono, 'I know just the person', and in came Bono with this very posh lady, full of life and full of questions. I struggled to my feet, re-engaged my tired brain and listened.

Firstly, she wanted to know if I had heard of the Parker family, who used to live at the Waen. Theirs was the very stone I had struggled with all afternoon to try and decipher. So I said, 'Follow me, and I will take you to see their grave.'

As we were walking down to the old yard in Felindre, her husband appeared and wanted to know where Beguildy Church was. I told him and he went off down the road with his camera to Beguildy and we went into the yard to look at the Parker headstone — at least the side I had cleaned. Since then, we have cleaned the other three sides of the headstone and sent the information over to America for them.

As they left, she handed me some papers which she said might be of interest to me. I thanked her and went back in the house to finish my 'rest' and take a look at them. Oh what a treasure! They were so interesting that I feel I must share them with you, and you will see the kind of tough, determined people who used to live around here nearly two hundred years ago.

A descendant of this Parker family, John Price, the son of a Parker daughter, married a Sarah Humphreys — the daughter of Elizabeth Humphreys, who was Elizabeth Williams before she married. John and Sarah were married in Beguildy Church in 1824 although they were both devout Baptists. Their geographical record of the area is interesting. 'The town of Beguildy is on the same latitude as Aberystwyth and is near the English border. A few miles up the road is the little town of Felindre.' Well, how about that! We've come up in the world a bit.

John and Sarah Price's first home was at the Waen — still the 'old house'. Most of their children were born there. Later they moved to Brynddu Farm, Llananno. I have been talking to Bill and Joan Watson who now live at Brynddu Farm, and they can remember an American couple calling on them about ten years ago. Bill and Joan had both been out drenching lambs, so were not very good-smelling company, but the American lady was thrilled to be there. 'At last,' she said, 'I have come home'. So we think she must have been a granddaughter of one of the younger daughters of Sarah and John Price. She was nearly 80 years old, and said that they had just celebrated their diamond wedding anniversary. A Blanche Price died in 1992. I wonder was this Blanche?

John and Sarah Price had twelve children altogether. In 1846, their first two sons, John who was then 21, and Edward, who was only 14, both emigrated to America. John had married Jane George, and other George sisters and their husbands joined them. They set sail from Liverpool on the ship *Niagara*, and landed in New York five weeks later. They then travelled up the Eerie Canal, through the Great Lakes and settled down in Wisconsin in an area later called The Welsh Prairie.

Having built their own houses and moved in, John and Edward then built a house for their parents. In 1856, John and Sarah Price with their nine children set out from Llananno, again to Liverpool, to start their long sea journey. Of course, by then some of the children would have been in their teens or early twenties. They too were five weeks at sea, and poor Sarah was again pregnant and was sick every day. Nearing the end of the long voyage she gave birth to a son, whom they named Samuel, but he died shortly after his birth and was buried at sea. Little Moses, aged just two, also died on that journey, and he too was buried at sea.

They landed in America — some say in Baltimore, Maryland and some say New York. They travelled by rail to the end of the line at Beaver Dam, Wisconsin. There they bought an oxen and a small wagon, on which they loaded all their belongings, including the family Bible and a Welsh brass and copper bed warmer with a long wooden handle. Sarah was allowed to ride as she was still too weak to walk. At last they arrived at their house on the edge of the Welsh Prairie, which John and Edward had built for them.

John and Sarah were still devout Baptists, but their nearest Baptist chapel was in Portage, a distance of twelve miles away. On many Sunday mornings, they would rise early and set out walking or sometimes travel by oxen and cart. They are both buried in the cemetery at Wyocena, Wisconsin.

Since writing this, I have been handed a piece of paper with the following on, so maybe emigrating to America was more common than I had thought —

In 1847, the following couples emigrated from around here:

Edward and Jane, Penybank, Llanbadarn Fynydd
William and Mary, Cwmgwyn Hall, Felindre
Mary and Richard Grovener, Llanbister
John and Mary Trow, Killowent, Felindre
Benjamin and Caroline Layton, Llanfihangel Rhydithon
John and Mary Swancott, Llanddewi

The general emigration officer was Rickards, Newtown. One of his brothers married a Thomas, The Criggin, Llananno — a sister to Jane, The Waen. The fares were:

	Australia	£12
	Brisbane	£14
Fast clipper to:		
	New Zealand	£11 11s. & £13 13s,
	Canada	£3
	U.S.A.	£3.10s

This price list was up in the window of their shop in Newtown.

The Waen under Mr. Bowen and Mr. Edward Davies

But now I must return to The Waen and its history. In the 1891 census we find that a William Bowen aged 50, his wife Mary 40, and their two sons, Thomas 13 and William 9, lived there. They also had two N.C.s or Nursing Children living with them — John Barrett 8, and his sister, Eliza Barrett, aged 6. The Bowen family would have been given a small amount of money from the Parish to help pay their bills. These little children had most probably lost their mother, possibly in childbirth, as so often happened in those days, and this money was given by the Church, or sometimes the Chapels, who in turn had been given annual sums of £5, £10, £20 or even £100 donated by the rich landowners to help with the poor of the parish.

By 1901 The Waen was recorded as empty, but there were already plans to build a new house. The Marpole family were the builders, and the bricks were handmade in the field under Fiddlers Green and carried up to the site by donkey-cart, which annoyed old Mr. Davies who was then living at Penfynon near Blaen-Nanty. The loud braying of the donkeys kept him awake at night.

The new house was large, with six bedrooms, and all the rooms had very high ceilings. It also had a cool cellar for storing food in summer — a good idea as there were no deep-freezers or fridges around then. There was also a stone slab on which to salt the pig.

However, over the years these bricks have proved to be not the best for keeping the wet out. When we arrived at The Waen in 1956 the front wall facing the west was covered in corrugated zinc, and painted red, but it was still a damp house. Also, the stone floor must have been laid directly onto the soil, because every so often a mole would leave an hwnt-y-twmp (mole hill) on the side of the hall and also in the dairy behind the hall.

The house was not finished until a couple of years after the 1901 census, and only then did the Davies family move in. Mr. Edward Davies was a Mochdre lad, and he had married Jane Thomas, a daughter from The Criggin, Llananno. Their first home was in Newport, South Wales, most probably having moved down there to find work in the coalmines, and where Sidney, their first child, was born. Later they moved back up to Radnorshire, but as their new house at the Waen was not ready, they moved into The Turgey. While at The Turgey, Millie and the twin boys — Edward and Vincent — were born. Margaret of Flirt (Criggin now) remembers hearing about Granny Morris going to The Turgey to look after twin boys. Granny Morris would be an auntie for Betty Lloyd, Carreg-y-frain. When The Waen was finished, Edward Davies and his family moved in.

Mr. Edward Davies who moved back up to Radnorshire and settled at The Waen. He became a very good supporter of Cwmgwyn Chapel

Around the same time, a Mr. Abraham Jones and his wife also decided to pack up the coalmines and move back to Radnorshire. Originally, they were both from Abbey-cwm-hir, but had moved down to South Wales to seek their fortune. This family lived firstly around Llanbister, then moved into the old house at The Waen for a short while, and subsequently to Windy Hall, where they lived for many years.

These two men — Mr. Jones and Mr. Davies — became very good friends and neighbours. Both were staunch Baptists and were very much involved in the buying of the little Wesleyan chapel at Cwmgwyn, and the building of the present larger Baptist chapel.

Mr. Edward Davies and his wife Jane had three more children while living at The Waen — Lilla, Irene and John. Sadly, when John was still very young, his mother died at the age of 44, and Millie and her younger sisters helped their dad to bring up the family.

I have been told many stories about the twin boys, Ned and Vin, while they were in their teens and later, but there is one I feel I can pass on. Their means of transport was a pushbike — as it was for most of the other young folk around in those days. Their father had a Ford — one of the first cars up the top end of the valley. To try to stop them from using the car, their father would take one wheel off and take it up to bed with him, but Mr. Rogers, Gwernerrin, also had the same make of car — and there were not many cars around in the valley. The twins must have had a very important date to keep one night, for they cycled down to Gwernerrin — a distance of over five miles — took a wheel off Mr. Rogers' car, cycled back up to the Waen and put the wheel on their dad's car, and away to go — probably to a dance somewhere around. Then when they returned in the early hours of the morning, they returned the wheel to Gwernerrin, cycled back home and up to bed. Boys, boys — were those girls really worth all that trouble?

They were also very good footballers and runners, as was their brother, Sidney, and would be found at many of the Sports for miles around. All three boys played football for the Felindre Football Team, when I hear it was one of the best anywhere around. They were good singers too, along with the rest of the family, and would take part in the Anniversary at Cwmgwyn.

The children grew up and got married, but they did not travel far to find their partners. Sidney, the oldest son, married Ethel of Windy Hall and they lived at Brickhouse for a while, and then moved to Owlbury, Churchstoke. They had three children — Doris, Sidney and Betty. These children and their families are still loyal to Cwmgwyn and come back to the Anniversary and other special services.

Millie, the oldest daughter, married Jack of Windy Hall, and they moved to the Dowke, Newcastle, Clun. They also had three children — Tilda, Jack and Trevor. Jack and Millie are both buried in the new yard in Felindre, together with Jack the son, his wife Gwyneth, and their baby son, John, grandson Jason, and granddaughter Julie, who died with her grandmother, Gwyneth, in a car crash. She was 13 years old. Trevor still comes back often to Cwmgwyn to the Anniversary and Songs of Praise. He and his wife have just celebrated their Golden Wedding.

The twin boys married two of the Reynolds sisters from the village. Edward married Irene and they lived at Brynmawr, or Brickhouse as it was then called.

They have two daughters, Gwyneth and Dorothy. Both these girls are very musical and would sing in the choir, and Dorothy played the organ for the Sunday School.

Gwyneth married Bryan McCann and they lived away for several years, but have returned to Lower Fiddlers Green to retire, and are both back in Cwmgwyn choir and the chapel. They have two daughters — Sandra, who lives in Australia; and Marcia, who has married George Wilding and lives at The Ddol, and they have two sons.

Dorothy married Gerald Scott and moved to Shrewsbury. Gerald worked on the railway. They have two sons, Graham and Robin, both good footballers but I haven't heard about their singing. Dorothy plays the organ in a large church near where they live. Irene, their mother, lived near Dorothy and only passed away in 2001.

Ruby Reynolds married Vin, one of the twin boys

Margaret, the Criggin, took Phoebe Reynolds and me down to see her when she was 95 and she was as bright as a button and could remember a lot of things about Cwmgwyn.

Vincent married Ruby Reynolds and they moved into The Waen. They had two children — John and Joyce. Ruby was a very good singer and when we moved to The Waen, Doug and Ruby used to sing duets at the chapel and in the Concert Party. Joyce had a most beautiful alto voice and although, after she married Percy Evans, she moved to Newtown, she would always come back and sing in the Anniversary and was a faithful and active member of the chapel right up to her sudden death.

I expect John would take part in the Anniversary when he was young but, as one gentleman told me, he was always up to the daundest mischief and, indeed, I have heard many stories about him but I expect you have, too. He died in 1987 aged 61, is buried in Felindre Chapel yard, and has left behind a lovely little family.

Joyce Davies, The Waen, with her friend Vaunda Brick

Lilla married John Wilding, The Ddol, and they had two sons

— Ronald, who joined the Navy but now lives in Newtown; and George, who married Marcia, a daughter for Gwyneth and Bryan, and they still live at The Ddol. Lilla was the organist at Cwmgwyn for many years. Both Lilla and John are buried in Felindre — John died in 1981 aged 75 and Lilla died in 1987 aged 84.

George is a deacon in the chapel and the whole family have been very helpful and generous with their time and money and also living so near, with the use of their tractor and other facilities.

Irene (Rene) married, firstly, Tom Reynolds, Llanllwyd and they lived at Cwmbugail. They had a son, Albert, who is now living in Knighton. Sadly Tom died in 1935 at the age of 35. Later Rene married Fred Lewis, The Hendre, and their first home was a little cottage by the side of the Wesleyan chapel, but tragedy struck again and their little cottage was burned down and they lost their little son, Wyndham, but Albert was staying away with his grandmother at Llanllwyd and was saved. Fred and Rene had two more children — Eileen and Edward. Eileen married Neville Huffer and they moved to Clunton, and Edward married Margaret Pugh of Nantypyllau, locally called Flirt. By this time, Fred and Rene had moved to the Criggin in Felindre and Edward and Margaret lived in part of the house, and are still there. They have two children, Amanda and David. Amanda has married Andrew Reynolds, Rhyd-y-Cwm and they live in part of the Criggin now with their three sons, and Margaret and Edward have moved to the other part. David married Joy and they have three daughters. David now lives in London.

Young John moved to Gwenlas and farmed there, but he was still a young lad, and life was very hard. His father joined him, and also his sister, Lilla, went to keep house for him. Some time later the father, Edward Davies, married Margaret Anne Jones, a widow from Blaen-Voil. Her husband, Jack Jones, had died some years before and is buried in the old yard in Felindre, along with a young son — but another son, also Jack, was out in service. This Margaret was a Tong girl from Llanbister Road, and when Edward Davies died in 1928, she went back to live with her mother and sister. She died in 1955 and is buried in the Gravel Chapel yard by her sister.

When Lilla was going to get married, she left Gwenlas and a May Hamer, the Cruchel, came as a housekeeper. Later John and May got married and farmed at Gwenlas for many years. John was a trustee at Cwmgwyn Chapel. They had four children — Dennis who married Audrey and they still live at Gwenlas; Alan who moved down to the New Forest

May Hamer and John Davies married in 1946

to his wife Jackie's home and worked down there; and the two girls, Gillian, who married John Thomas, the Tanhouse, and they still live at Dolau; and Ruth, who married a solicitor and they live just outside Aberystwyth. May is still alive and lives in Llandrindod, but John died several years ago and is buried in Maesyrhelem. All the Gwenlas children are good singers, even the next generation, so I hear.

And that is a brief history of the Davies family, The Waen. Little did Edward Davies think, when he moved back up to Radnorshire from the coalmines in South Wales, that he and his family would help to bring the Cwmgwyn area to life, and through his children and grandchildren would leave a lasting legacy of music and song which still carries on a hundred years later.

Sadly in 1928, he died at the age of 60, and is buried with his wife Jane in the old yard in Felindre. This was another tragedy, as the cause of his death was a septic hand, and as there were no antibiotics around in those days, it quickly turned to septicemia, and that is a killer even today if not treated in time. There is a plaque on the wall in Cwmgwyn Chapel to his memory — the little chapel he helped to build and to which he and his family gave a lifetime of hard work, love and singing.

The Waen under the Thomas family

In March 1956, Doug and I moved to The Waen, with David our four months old baby. It was Newtown March Fair, and the rain was coming down in torrents. At that time there was no road down from the crossroads up by Blaen-Nanty, so we had to go right out to the pool on the hill, then down to Cwmgwyn kiosk and up the pitch by the pool — an extra couple of miles. I was travelling in the lorry with David on my knee — no car seats or seat belts in those days. As we came to the pool on the hill, there was a roadblock, and we were stopped by the police. The driver had to show his driving licence, then as we came to the bottom of the hill, we were stopped again by a policeman. I was beginning to wonder what sort of an area we were coming to live in, and it all looked so wild and bleak with not a house in sight! Later we were told that two local men were driving their vans to market without a licence, and both were caught that day.

Doug had gone ahead in the van to light the fire and warm the house up a little. He had a roaring fire in the coalhouse — there was no grate in the living

The Waen when we first moved in — with its corrugated zinc covering the front west-facing wall and painted red. I am with David and his cousin Heather

room — but with two outside doors and a very large chimney, most of the heat was going straight up the chimney. And so, with no electric, no telephone, no water in the house, and not much of anything else, we started our new life at The Waen. We had both been used to all the mod. cons. for at least ten years, but we could both remember the days before all these amenities and thought we could easily cope with it. I really did not think that life could be so hard. How we lived — or even survived — that first year, I do not know, and I became pregnant again. My doctor had given me some wonderful new pills to help stop the dreaded 'morning sickness'. However, in the November our second son was born, but was recorded as 'still born'. Many years later we discovered that I had been given the thalidomide drug, and that our baby was deformed. It's frightening to think what damage one small pill can do, especially to an unborn child.

Gillian and Ruth often used to ride their ponies up to the Waen at weekends and holidays, and would take David for rides

Life began to get better the next year. We had a grant to improve our house, so we had a new roof, new windows, and new ceilings in all the bedrooms — we had only been able to use the large room above the coalhouse. The other rooms had windows out, and ceilings falling down on rough weather. We now had a bathroom with hot and cold water and a toilet — so no more running up the garden to the rather posh two-seater! We also had a new Rayburn, so at least we had a warm house

David and John in Llanbadarn Sports carnival as the Lone Ranger and Tonto. They are riding Gillian's and Ruth's ponies and wearing outfits sent over from America by Doug's Auntie Minnie

and hot water, and I could cook and roast a dinner. Before it had only been a frying pan, a large black pot with a handle over the top, and a fountain — all hanging above the open fire. We also moved out of that cold, draughty old coalhouse, but still no electric or telephone.

In February of the next year, John was born in our new bathroom!! We had been blocked in with snow for a whole week, but on the Sunday evening Doug managed

The Waen after our first alterations

to get out to Llanbadarn to get the midwife, Mrs. Clee. He went down across the hill to Gwenlas, then out to Llanbadarn on our old grey Fergie tractor, so Mrs. Clee arrived half frozen to death, poor soul. How brave and strong they were in those days to even set out on such weather, as there would be no cab or shelter on those old tractors — just hang on for dear life and hope for the best!

Back in those days I think we used to have more rough winters, with heavy falls of snow. The road from Cwmgwyn up past the Cider House would fill up with snow very quickly. The wind would blow the dry snow off the open fields, and it would get caught in the road between the hedges. In the early days, the only method of clearing a way through was by man-and-shovel power, and this was a hard, slow job. Later, the snow-ploughs and blowers

Brisbane's lorry has brought extra men to help our local roadman clear the road to Newtown. Jack of Cork (on the right) and Tom James (kneeling) are two of the local men

A snow-storm up on the hill near Cider House in 1995

came on the market, so at least a one-way traffic road could be cut through the snow much quicker. This was a sight to see, as it was like a tunnel through the snow, and I have heard of folk taking a trip up there just to see it. If you were caught in a real blizzard up on the top, it was a frightening experience — as well I know, but I was lucky enough to reverse back to the Cider House and turn, then go back to Dolfor and back home via Crossgates and Knighton — a long way round but we got home.

Doug used to be called out even in the middle of the night sometimes, to pull a traveller out of a snowdrift with the tractor, and set them back down the road they had just come on. Some, when they were pulled out, would want to keep going on up the hill, but Doug told them he would not come out again when they were stuck, and stuck they would have been before they got to Dolfor.

Joan and Bill, The Garn, have many stories to tell of rescuing people stranded out on the top roads. Even our son, David, who now lives at The Waen, has been called out several times to help people, and has had to get the tractor to pull them out, but these days the tractors have a cab on, so it is not nearly such a cold job. We do seem to be getting milder winters just lately — but watch out now I've said this.

Our next three boys were born in hospital in the spring or summer, and then at last we had our little girl in Knighton Hospital. Doctor Davies delivered her, and he told me that the telephone lines were all buzzing with excitement up the valley.

In the June of our first year at The Waen, we were both on the platform at Cwmgwyn singing in the choir. Doug also sang in duets and quartets. He had a good and true voice, and firstly he sang duets with Ruby Davies, who used to live at The Waen. A few years later he started to sing with Joan Lewis, The Garn, and they were singing together for nearly thirty years, right up to the time of his death.

We did not get the electric to The Waen until after our fourth son, Graham, was born. Just imagine washing all those nappies by hand — no throw-aways in those days — then boiling them in the big black pot on the Rayburn. Nappies had

The old water wheel at Gwenlas. John had managed to get the old wheel working and it would generate enough electricity to drive the television

to be whiter than white before you hung them on the line — and who on earth saw them up there? But they were always boiled.

Doug missed the television for football and boxing when we first went to The Waen, so he used to go down to Gwenlas most Saturday nights to watch. John, who was the youngest son for Edward Davies, The Waen, had managed to get the old water-wheel working, and it would generate enough electricity to drive the telly.

Our children were growing up fast, and as we lived so far out in the wilds, they needed trans-

The Thomas family in 1971. Helen Barrett displayed this once in our village hall with the caption 'Clarice has even matched the boys' shirts to the wall-paper'!

port to get them to meetings and clubs. They were in the Young Farmers' Club and one or other would have a football or rugger match to go to. By this time I had passed my test so we bought Ivor Reynolds, The Vron's old navy Wolseley car, so some weekends we would both be out chauffeuring them around. I wanted them all to have some music, so I would take the four boys over to Olwen Bowen in Llanbister and they had one hour to share!

In the late 1960s and early '70s we were told to diversify, as it was getting harder to make money at farming. We had been looking into the potato market, and had even got all the forms ready to fill in, when the Director of Education from Llandrindod came to The Waen and asked — no, pleaded with me to go back to teaching. It was to be just afternoons to start with at Llanbister School. Everyone at home thought this was a very good idea, so the potato forms went into the bin and I became the potato crop! Some time later the Council houses in Knucklas were built, and the children — and there were many — were transported to Beguildy School, so I was asked to go and help there.

When I went back into teaching after Dianne was born, I first had a young girl from the Llaithddu — a Joyce Hardwick — to look after her. Joyce's delight was to dress Dianne in pretty clothes, but she looked after her well. After her, Sue Deakin from Howey came. Sue would also look after Dianne well, but her delight was to cook a good dinner for Doug with plenty left for the boys when they came home from school. Sue was a qualified nurse and she had a job in New Zealand to go to, so she was only with us just over a year. She is still in New Zealand and Dianne, Brian and I have been over to see her and her family.

After Sue, we had Danish au pair girls, and Doug also had a Danish lad to help on the farm, so we became very friendly with several Danish families, all connected with farming. One year we all went over to Denmark in our new Maxi car. We took Doug's mother too, so that made nine of us, but we all got in the Maxi and had a wonderful time. There were no seat belts then, and his Mum even nursed Dianne on her knee in the front seat, and there were always two or three boys in the boot — with the shelf taken out — and most of our luggage had to go on the roof rack.

At about this time we formed the Dolithon Choir, and this was a turning point in our lives. We could both go out together and leave our au pair to look after Dianne and the boys. In the beginning, I had to play the piano but, as it was usually hymn tunes, I could just about manage. Then we began to enter and often win at local eisteddfodau, so we

Our Danish au pair girls with Dianne

Rebe Brick busy cooking on an open fire — no posh barbeques in those days

Dianne and I up at the Garn with Auntie Nancy, Joan and Thelma. This photograph and that opposite were printed in the Danes' yearbook

asked Margaret Lewis, the Criggin, to join us and be our pianist and I became the conductor, and we have both been doing these jobs for the past thirty years.

The head of the Agricultural College, where, by this time, our Danish lad was a student, asked if he could bring three busloads of students over for a week at the end of their college course. So started some wonderful exchange trips, with our choir and friends going over to Denmark, and then everyone came to The Waen to help with this great gang of Danes. Usually they would stay with us for three or four days, camping out in the fields, then they would move down to Builth and visit the Royal Welsh Show, then finish their week with a day in London.

After we had moved down to the village, they came for a couple more years. Once we

A few Danes at the barbecue at the Village Hall

cleared out the big building at the Criggin and we fed them in there and also sang for them. Mr. Ed. had made a wonderful outside toilet for them — seat and all! The last time they came we had a barbeque in the Village Hall grounds for them. We had killed and dressed three lambs, as well as boxes of sausages, baked potatoes and bread rolls by the dozens. After all the food had disappeared, the choir stood on the cesspit and we sang for them. The Danes loved our four-part harmony singing.

Doug was also involved in the Sports at Felindre when it was one of the biggest sports anywhere around. He and his best friend, Arthur Brick, were also loyal supporters of our local tug-of-war team, and would go with them whenever they could. They went to Ireland twice, and Italy and Holland, as well as places in this country.

All through the years, we have never failed to be on the platform at Cwmgwyn. Doug also joined the Newtown Male Voice Choir, and later the Rhayader and District Male Voice Choir, and has been to the Royal Albert Hall in London singing with the Thousand Welsh Male Voice Choirs on several occasions. These were wonderful weekends, and often some of our little Dolithon Choir would come with us and we would have a great time. We would also try to fit in a show, and a bit of window-shopping!

The Danes with their three buses at the Royal Welsh Show

Our five boys in Lego land in Denmark around 1970

61

I have also had some exciting moments. I went up in a hot-air balloon — a truly wonderful trip — thanks to friends of Edward and Margaret, the Criggin. Then I won a trip in a micro-light, but didn't care too much for that. When I left teaching, I was given a ticket for a two-hour flight on Concorde and this again was wonderful, especially as a busload of friends came up to London with me. I have also had a holiday of a lifetime staying with Sue in New Zealand. Dianne and Brian had already been out there for six months, then all three of us went to Australia, back-

Doug and Mr. Anderson, head of the agricultural college in Denmark, and three bus loads of students. Lower Fiddler's Green can be seen in the distance of the top photograph

Our silver wedding in 1979, our only anniversary celebration

packing, but we travelled the East side — Sydney, Melbourne, Adelaide, Ayres Rock, Alice Springs, then up to the Barrier Reef. Then we stayed ten days in America, and went to Disneyland, Universal Studios, saw the old *Queen Mary* and the Spruce Goose, and also visited Doug's Auntie Minnie, and then we came back home, stony broke but happy!

In July 1991, very sadly Doug died, after being told that he had cancer more than nine years before — but what a nine years. We did not waste a minute, and he was well for most of that time. His death was a great loss to many, as well as to our family, and my way of coping was to carry on as near to normal as possible, and keep busy. The hardest was the singing but I was back with the little choir within the twelve months, and also Cwmgwyn. That, I'm sure, would have been what he would have wanted.

Now I'm afraid I have gone beyond us living at The Waen, but he was always 'Doug, The Waen', so I felt it was right to keep going to the end of his days.

The Waen had changed hands several years before. David had married Jackie Farmer in February 1978. She was a Knighton girl and at that time a hairdresser. Their first home was Brickhouse, as we were still at The Waen. Then in the December,

Dianne, me and Brian ready to leave America after a holiday of a lifetime

*Back row: Alan, Gemma, Vicky, Kate.
Front row: David, Marc, Jackie*

John and Frances with George, Lily and Arthur

we all moved down to The Stores in the village and David and Jackie moved into The Waen. They now have five children — Alan, Gemma, Vicky, Kate and Marc.

Karen and Robert

John married Frances Price, also a Knighton girl, and they live on the outskirts of the town. Frances is a dental hygienist and John, with his brother Graham, has started up a small factory in Knighton, making electrical control systems for industry. They had three children, George, Lily, and Arthur.

Robert married Karen, a London girl, and they have bought an old farmhouse and buildings in Brittany, France, and with a lot of hard work and a little help from his brothers, they have turned it into a rather large and popular holiday resort. They have also bought a couple of smaller properties and are repairing these.

Graham lived in Hastings for many years and has a son, Evan, who is now a teenager. Graham has now moved up to Knighton with his present partner Maureen, and is in the factory with John.

Graham and Maureen, and Graham's son Evan

Brian married a local girl Yvonne Reynolds, Black House. Yvonne is a teacher and Brian an accountant. They have both worked in London and Shrewsbury, but have now moved back to Felindre and live in part of The Stores — next door to my granny flat. They have two children, Jamie and Megan.

Dianne became a doctor and married a doctor — Robert Gilmore from Kent. They both trained in Cardiff, but now have moved to Kent and live near his family. They have three children, Bethan, Owen and Angharad. They are now both G.P.s and work in Bearsted.

Brian and Yvonne with Megan and Jamie

Robert and Dianne with Bethan, Owen and Angharad

David and Jackie continued to live and work much the same as we had. They farmed Brickhouse and The Waen. Their children went to Beguildy School, then on to John Beddoes, Presteigne — just as ours had done.

David, and Jackie when she could, liked to go out and play darts and dominoes, whereas we had gone out singing, although Doug also enjoyed his pub games when he had time.

Then one dreadful day in February 2001, life changed completely for the family. Jackie and Alan had gone to work in the Radnor Hills bottled water plant, and the rest of the children had gone to school, leaving David at home alone.

About a week before, David had bought a few lambs from market, and had shut them in the building for a few days. On this Tuesday he decided to let them out to join the other sheep in the field, when he noticed two of them a little lame. As there were a few cases of foot and mouth in the country already, he rang the vet at once, and it was confirmed very quickly as the disease.

David rang Jackie and Alan, and also both schools. No one was allowed home, and so we quickly made arrangements for the children to stay elsewhere. Two

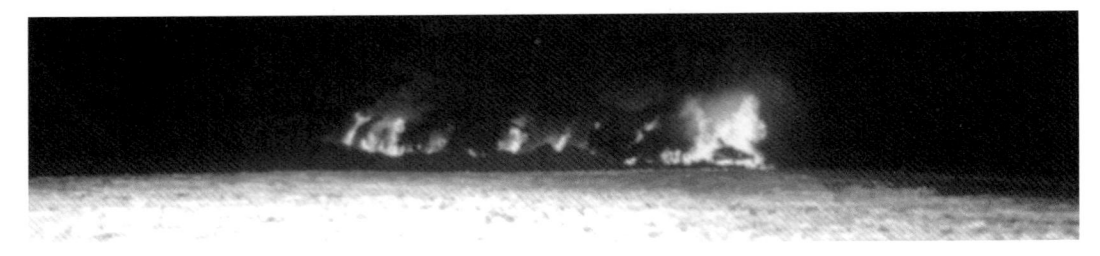

During the outbreak of Foot and Mouth the animals were shot, burned and buried. The fire burned for days, the smell lingered for weeks and the memory lives on

stayed with their Nan, Rose Farmer, in Knighton and the other three stayed with me at the shop. Jackie wanted to go home to be with and help David through the terrible ordeal that was before them, so she had to sign a form saying that she would not leave the farm until they were given the 'all clear'.

We had to send food and post in boxes up to the end of the lane for them. There was a policeman on duty checking everything and everybody. Then they had to send schoolbooks and clothes down for the children — again in boxes left at the end of the lane for us to collect. The schoolchildren had left home that Tuesday morning with books and clothes for only one day. What a time it was for us all, but far worse for David and Jackie. They had to watch and even help to round up all their sheep and cattle to be shot, burned and buried in the field just below the house — only seven ponies and two dogs left.

They had the 'all clear' six weeks later, and the children could go home and the parents could come out at last. David was not allowed to re-stock for another nine months while all the buildings and land were disinfected. By this time, he had decided not to go back into farming for the moment, so he has 'let' most of the land to a neighbouring farmer and joined his brothers in the factory in Knighton.

A lone calf at Waen Farm during Foot and Mouth. This little picture in our local paper summed it all up: sadness and despair

The family still live at The Waen, and have kept their ponies and dogs. Farming these days is not a very profitable way of making a living, especially on the smaller farms, and there is so much paperwork and form filling, by law, to be done. What would our fathers and forefathers have thought if they were told that even the animals these days need 'passports'. Perhaps David will give it another go in the future, especially if Marc shows an interest in farming.

Life at The Waen was never easy, especially in the beginning, but I look back now and think that with all those boys and our little girl, who was quite a little tomboy, it was not such a bad place to bring up a family. There was plenty of room outside, or in the buildings, for them to play and at least get from under my feet for a while, but I am amazed that we had no major catastrophes or broken bones. Indeed, it was poor Doug who had the most serious accidents, and I feel sometimes that they were the cause of his troubles in later life.

One of the biggest changes at The Waen while we were there was in the 1960s when the electricity and the telephones came, whilst the roads were improved with many more cars and vans using them.

Today, of course, there are big changes taking place again with computers, the Internet and the mobile phone. Sometimes when I have several children and grandchildren in my kitchen and they are all talking, I feel as if I am in a different world, and half the time I don't even know, or understand, what they are talking about.

So that's the modern Thomas family, The Waen and I'll finish here, and go and get out my old violin!

Windy Hall

This was most probably a little *ty-un-nos*, as its name implies for such homes were often called grand names, and also from its size we see from the photograph. It was situated on the right-hand side of the road going up from the Waen turn to the Llanbadarn road. When we first moved to the Waen in 1956, there was no road there so we would have to go to the pool on the hill, then down to Cwmgwyn and back up to the Waen.

In the 1891 census, farmer Richard Jones 39, his wife Emily 40, and their son James, lived there with Sarah Brown, step-daughter, and John Richards, servant. By 1901 they had all moved away and Abraham L. Jones 36, his wife Sarah 35, and Abraham 14, Bertha 11, John (Jack) 8, Ethel 5, and Elsie, ten months, lived there, having moved from the old house at the Waen where they lived for a very short while. This couple were originally both from Abbey-cwm-hir, but had moved down to South Wales, most probably to the coalmines, as did a lot of young couples in those days. I hear that Sarah Jones was related to Mrs. Betty Jones, Llangurig, who is married to Richard

Mr. Abraham Jones

Jones, the singer. A few years ago, Richard came to Cwmgwyn, to conduct our Songs of Praise.

This was the Abraham Jones, who with Edward Davies, the Waen, had been very involved in the buying of the little Wesleyan chapel at Cwmgwyn and the building of the extension, making a much larger Baptist chapel in 1908. He was also superintendent of the Sunday School for forty years and, for many of those years he had worked hard trying to keep the young lads quiet and in order on the Anniversary days.

Abraham and Sarah had five children, and they were all involved in Cwmgwyn Chapel, as were the Davies family, the Waen, and both fathers were very good friends and neighbours. Some of the children did not travel very far to find their partners. Jack, of Windy Hall, married Millie of the Waen, and they set up home at the Dowke, Newcastle. They had three children — Tilda, who lives in Newtown, and Jack who married Gwyneth. They both died young and

Mr. and Mrs. A. Jones

Iris Lloyd (The Culvert) outside Windy Hall

From left to right: young Jack (Windy Hall), Cliff James (Fiddlers Green), Reuban Morgan (Fiddlers Green), Abraham Jones (Windy Hall)

are buried in Felindre yard, together with a baby son and grandson, then tragically, a couple of years ago, a granddaughter, who died with Gwyneth, her grandmother in a car crash. Their third child, Trevor, still comes back to Cwmgwyn for the Anniversary and Songs of Praise.

Then Sidney, The Waen, married Ethel of Windy Hall, and their first home was Brickhouse, later moving to Oldbury, Churchstoke. This couple had three children — Doris, who is now 90 years old; Betty, who married Derek Redge and now lives in Bishops Castle; and Sidney.

Bertha of Windy Hall, married Albert Davies, The Gwridd,

From left to right: Margaret Lewis, Dorothy Scott (Brickhouse), Cliff James and Doris Jones (who married Trevor of Windy Hall) the Anchor, who lived to be 102 years old. They had two daughters — Mrs. Dorothy Hudson, Cow Hall; and Mrs. Elsie Greenall, who is married to a finance broker in Ludlow.

I hear that Abraham, the oldest son, emigrated to Ontario, Canada, and married a Canadian girl, Evelyn, and they had three children. Abraham joined the Canadian Army and fought in the Second World War. They lived very near Detroit on the U.S.A. border. Some of his children keep in touch, so perhaps we shall have more details about him.

Elsie, the youngest daughter of Windy Hall, died in childbirth, as sadly so often happened in those days. Sarah, the mother, died young and was buried in the old yard at Felindre in 1918, aged 53. Abraham, her husband, continued living at Windy Hall for many years, then he moved to Rose Villa, Bwlchsarnau, and died there in 1953, aged 90. He is buried with his wife in Felindre, next to the Davieses, The Waen, side by side, as they had lived for most of their lives.

After we moved to the Waen, a brother and sister came to Windy Hall and kept pigs and poultry, but I think they left after a couple of years, and it has been empty ever since.

Today there is little trace of it left.

Fiddlers Green

In order to give you some of the early history of Fiddlers Green, I would like to print, with permission from the *County Times*, part of an article written by Cynric Mytton-Davies in 1972. Many of you will remember him.

There is a photograph of Cwmgwyn Chapel on the front page, taken by the paper's photographer, Donald Griffiths. These two men used to go out and about, looking for interesting stories. Cynric writes:

> One day, we were returning to Newtown up the Teme valley, and when we came to the foot of the Kerry Hills, where the road zig-zags up on to the moors, I noticed a tiny Chapel, which you see a little way down a side track, and commented as to how such places of worship came to be built in such lonely and out of the way places, and whether it was because of the Five Mile Act in the days of intolerance.

Don's response surprised Cynric: 'My great-great-grandmother used to worship there — she could have told us'.

Later, Don came to me with an unexpected invitation. His grandmother — Naomi Morgan's granddaughter — remembered visiting her at Fiddlers Green when she was a girl, and could tell me about the Cwmgwyn Chapel if I cared to look in and see her. It was hard to believe that Mrs. Jane Griffiths was in her '80s when I visited her in the 1970s. In every respect, one would have counted her twenty years younger. However, she was born in 1888, and at the turn of the century, she was about 12 years old. She used to go and stay with her grandmother at Fiddlers Green.

Naomi and Richard Morgan's children and sons-in-law.
From left to right. Back row: Jane Morgan, Elizabeth Morgan, John Mills,
Maria Mills (née Morgan)
Front row: Kate Morgan, John Davies, Annie Davies (née Morgan), Reuben Morgan.
Three of their children are absent from the photograph

The journey there from her home in Kerry, in the company of her sister, was eventful and exciting. Her mother, born Fanny Morgan, but who became Fanny Powell on her marriage to Edward Powell, lived in Kerry and would take the children in to Newtown on foot to meet their grandmother. Naomi used to drive into town in her donkey cart, which she would leave in the Sun yard by the Market Vaults, and there she would meet the girls after she had finished her shopping, and would set off back to Fiddlers Green with the children beside her.

But when they got to The Crugyn, the hairpin bend just above Dolfor, she would get down from the cart and set off walking across the fields, leaving the donkey to carry on, knowing that he knew the way. Then she would wait for the donkey and children at the Black Gate, and rejoin them when they caught up. Either she enjoyed the walk, or did this as a diversion for the children, we do not know, but they certainly never forgot it.

Jane Griffiths recalls her grandmother explaining the strange name of Fiddlers Green. It was supposed to be a small enclosure of very green grass nearby, surrounded by trees. Here, she told them, the fairies used to dance to music provided by a fairy fiddler, and this enclosure was his green. The legend of the *Tilwyth Teg*, or the Little People, contained many stories of fairies dancing in green circles or patches, at times enticing mortals to join them. If ever that happened, the mortal would pass what seemed like a mere half hour, but which in mortal time was many years, so that he would return to a world where he knew no-one and no-one knew him.

Naomi and her husband, Richard, attended Cwmgwyn Chapel after it had been bought by the Baptist denomination. Before that, houses were used as places of worship and Fiddlers Green could well have been one. Windy Hall and The Gravel were also often used.

Naomi used to tell her grandchildren about the burials from Cwmgwyn and the area around. As there was no burial ground at Cwmgwyn, everyone from that area had to be buried in Felindre Baptist Chapel yard, or in Beguildy Church yard. The funeral procession would be on foot, with relays of bearers to carry the coffin the four miles to the graveyard. Often it would be evening when they arrived and in wintertime it would be dark, so the burial service would take place by candlelight.

Mrs. Griffiths remembers the new Waen being built, with the bricks manufactured locally from the clay in the ground, and processed in a kiln under Fiddlers Green, but all traces of this have vanished now.

She also remembers her grandmother making butter, with a wooden shaft moving up and down in a wooden barrel, and the goose being allowed to lay her eggs in a nest under the stairs in the back kitchen. She would be allowed out every day for a short while, then back in to sit on her eggs until they hatched. Geese, in those days, were looked after very well, as they were a good source of money later on as Christmastime drew near.

Naomi died in 1918 aged 81, and Richard died in 1933 aged 86. The last of Naomi Morgan's descendants to live at Fiddlers Green was Laura Jane and her husband Thomas James, who had come up from the coalmines in South Wales. His sister Mary Ann, had also come up with him and she later married Sam Reynolds. Two of their daughters, Irene and Ruby married the twin boys from The Waen — Ned and Vin.

Laura Jane and Thomas James lived at Fiddlers Green and had four children — Thomas Reuben (Jim as we knew him, who had married Dorothy in the village); Beatie, who married and moved away; Kate Naomi, who lived in Knucklas; and Clifford who, although he was always very lame, used to drive a lorry for Nicholls, Llanddewi. I can remember that during the wartime he would drive a lorry around the farms collecting eggs and rabbits, which he would then take to Birmingham, or wherever they had to go. Since retiring, he has moved to Llandrindod, and drives out to Cwmgwyn every Sunday that there is a service, and even in 2005 I have just heard news of him. He is in hospital and has had his one leg amputated, but

Laura Jane Morgan and Thomas James, the parents of the four children — Beatie, Cliff, Kitty and Jim — in the photograph below

he is still very cheerful and positive, and is looking forward to getting back at the wheel of a new car and driving out to Cwmgwyn again.

Jane and Tom, their parents, moved to Dolfrynog, and ended their days there. They were both loyal to Cwmgwyn, and Jane would play the organ if needed. She was also a good alto singer and was always in the choir. She

Fiddlers Green, built by Ron Evans in the 1960s

died in 1956 aged 67, and Tom died in 1959 aged 69, and both are buried in Felindre. Fiddlers Green was left empty for many years.

Then one Felindre Sports day in the mid 1960s, I had taken my boys home from the Sports quite early, as they were all still young, when a motorbike and sidecar came into the yard at The Waen. They were a family from the Midlands looking for Fiddlers Green — Ron Evans; his partly crippled wife Anne, who had suffered from poliomyelitis when she was a child, was on the back of the bike with Ron; and their three young children — Wendy, Judy and Robert — were in the sidecar, as well as a tent and some camping equipment. What a brave little family they were!

At that time, I had Brickhouse as a holiday home, so they lived there while Ron bought the old Fiddlers Green, demolished it, and built their new bungalow on the site. Then Ron set up a market garden business, which had always been his dream. Some time later Ron built a little Woolaway bungalow for Anne's parents, and both families were happy for several years.

Then the health of Mr. and Mrs. Spillsbury, Anne's parents, began to deteriorate, and they moved back to Newtown, where they had a son still living, and so the little Woolaway bungalow was put on the market. Ron and Anne also had problems. I think we must have had one of our very bad winters and they lost most of their greenhouses in a terrible windstorm. In addition, the height of Fiddlers Green was against him for market gardening, so they sold up and, sadly, the couple split up. Anne and the children moved to Knighton and Ron went in for market gardening again, but this time nearer the Herefordshire border.

Fiddlers Green was then sold to Mr. and Mrs. Leason and their two children, Joanne and Graham. Mr. Leason had work in Newtown, but they only stayed a

Chris and Lyndsey French with their children David, Helen, Rhian and Anna

couple of years. Then they bought a smallholding on a little island just off the coast of the Orkneys, but I hear they are now back on the mainland, but still in the north of Scotland.

Next came Mr. and Mrs. Chris French and their four children, David, Helen, Rhian and Anna. Chris was an electronics engineer in Newtown and they stayed for several years, joining in the activities of the valley. Chris's work took him further and further away, so they moved to Shrewsbury, chiefly because of our road problems in that hilly area, especially in wintertime. They still keep in touch with several families in the valley.

Fiddlers Green was now bought by Mr. and Mrs. Wyke. He had been an airline pilot, so they travelled to many parts of the world. Their home was in St. Albans, and they had been coming out to Selley Hall, Llanfair Waterdine, for holidays with Mary and Llewelyn Morgan for many years. Since coming to Fiddlers Green, Rita has bought a spinning wheel and with a little tuition from Lesley Schofield, has taught herself to spin. She uses the sheep's wool from Bill Barnett, The Rhuvid, and David Thomas, The Waen, and has been busy making jumpers, scarves and hats for the families around. I think Naomi Morgan would have loved to meet you Rita, as of course, in those days they had to be self-sufficient and make use of the raw materials that were to hand, but I think you would not have enjoyed living in Naomi's day with no electric or telephone and no mod. cons. — indeed none of us would these days, but perhaps they were as happy then as we are today.

Rita has now sent a note to me with a little more history, which she has researched. She found in an old Oxford English Dictionary the meaning of the name, Fiddlers Green. It was a 'Sailors Elysium' in Greek mythology, where wine, women and song featured predominately. Fiddlers Green was where the James family lived, so what do you think of that, Cliff? (We always knew you were a 'rum-un'.) There is evidence of an even earlier house on the bottom side of the road, which used to have many trees growing around, but they all blew down one very stormy night way back in the early 1920s. This site is a water meadow now, and probably used to flood, so perhaps that's where the sailors come in to Fiddlers Green.

Up until the early 1950s, when the James family moved to Dolfrynog, it was still a small farm, but land was sold to The Waen, and when Ron Evans bought it, only seven acres remained. Rita says that when they bought it in 1988, it was only four and a half acres; the rest was part of Lower Fiddlers Green. There were still signs of the market garden and several unusual conifers could be seen. There is also a heather called Fiddlers Gold on the market today, which is said to have been cultivated at Fiddlers Green, but most of the heathers were destroyed by goats kept by a subsequent owner.

Rita's husband sadly died in 2002 and Rita has now moved down to Beguildy village with a few more people around than up at Fiddlers Green. Denise Hobbs and her partner, Andy Sinclair, have bought the property with its few acres of land. This couple run a little business from home as independent distributors for Forever Living Products Ltd. They also breed border terriers and keep 'love birds' and ponies. They enjoy riding for pleasure. Years gone by, many ponies were kept and used as the main form of transport, either riding or pulling traps, carts or wagons. Today we have vehicles of all sorts, shapes and sizes, but horsepower often measures their 'pulling' strength.

It's good to hear of pony riding being enjoyed up in these rather wild, hilly areas. Last year four ladies from the Cwmgwyn area, accompanied by a dog, rode from the coast near Harlech, then followed the old drovers' road right across to Cwmgwyn. They were Mrs. Marcia Wilding, The Ddol; Mrs. Frances Morris, Pound Gate; her daughter Mrs. Mair Stephens, Hafod Fadog, and Rhona Barnett, The Rhuvid. They enjoyed their ride very much, so perhaps the folk living around here a hundred years ago did not have such a bad life, after all.

The area around Fiddlers Green is very good for birds, and over eighty species have been observed, including the Red Kite and other birds of prey.

Lower Fiddlers Green

In the mid 1960s, Ron Evans had bought Fiddlers Green, demolished the old house and built a new bungalow on the same site for his wife Anne and family. He also set up a market garden, and when the business was going well he had a little Woolaway bungalow built lower down in his field and Anne's parents came to live in it. These little bungalows were very popular in the country areas at that time. They were prefabricated houses, made in sections in factories and brought out to the prepared site, where they were assembled quite quickly. These were comparatively low-cost, and many were built as retirement homes for a farmer and his wife, so that the son and his wife could move into the farmhouse. Sometimes they were built as farm workers' cottages.

When Mr. and Mrs. Spillsbury's health started to deteriorate, they decided to move back to Newtown where one of their children was still living, and Lower Fiddlers Green was put on the market. Bryan and Gwyneth McCann bought it, but did not move until he had retired from the police force a year or so later, in 1978.

Lower Fiddlers Green with Mr. and Mrs. Spillsbury out in the garden. This was a Woolaway bungalow, prefabricated and brought out to the prepared site

Both Bryan and Gwyneth were coming to an area they both knew very well. Gwyneth was born at Brickhouse and was a daughter for Irene and Ned Davies, and a granddaughter for Mr. Edward Davies, The Waen, and Bryan was a Newtown lad. Gwyneth was soon back in Cwmgwyn Chapel and in the choir, and Bryan also joined the choir. Some time later, they both joined the chapel, and have been very involved in the repairs and renovations of the chapel during the past few years.

Gwyneth with their two girls and one of Dorothy's boys, with Bryan and Ned by the cart

They are both senior citizens, but keep themselves very fit and active. Gwyneth enjoys walking and cycling and Bryan enjoys working, and has found a few more jobs at the chapel, which he must see to. They both have good voices and enjoy singing. They attend several Songs of Praise or singing festivals in the area.

Bryan is chairman of the chapel now, and Gwyneth is our treasurer, so both are very much involved in its running, just as Gwyneth's grandfather was over one hundred years ago.

Brickhouse or Bryn-mawr

This is a little cottage up on the hill above The Waen, and has, for many years, been connected with The Waen.

In the 1891 census we find George Morgan 21, his wife Elizabeth 24, and their twin boys, Richard and George, aged 2, and judging by their names, they were descendants of Richard and Naomi Morgan of Fiddlers Green.

Don Griffiths, the photographer for the *Mid Wales Journal*, has written to me to say that he remembers going to Brickhouse to celebrate the Diamond Wedding of his grandparents. I would think that they would be Naomi and Richard, although Don says that Mrs. Brick, Cefn-bedw was there, as she was his grandmother's best friend, so maybe I am a generation out! I find it very hard to slot people into the right generation, especially when some of the older folk live to be a big age.

In the 1901 census, George Morris 29, Winnie 23, and Thomas aged 1, lived there. In 1903 a Mr. Arthur Morris was on the Building Committee of Cwmgwyn Chapel, and his address was given as Brickhouse.

Some time later, Sidney Davies, The Waen, (the oldest son), married Ethel Jones of Windy Hall, and their first home was Brickhouse. Later, they moved to Oldbury in Churchstoke.

The next couple to live at Brickhouse was the young Edward Davies, one of the twins from The Waen and a brother to Sydney. Ned, as he was called, had married Irene Reynolds from the village. This couple had two daughters, Gwyneth and Dorothy, and they were all — parents and daughters — very good singers and very good supporters of Cwmgwyn Chapel. At one time, Ned was the conductor of Cwmgwyn choir, in which mother and both daughters sang. Also, Dorothy was the main organist for the Sunday School.

Irene Reynolds married Edward Davies (The Waen), and lived at the Brickhouse

Brickhouse, taken from up on the road in the 1950s

Then Gwyneth married Bryan McCann, who was a Newtown lad, and they moved away. Brian was in the police force, so had to go where his work was. They had two daughters — Sandra, who lives in Australia — and Marcia, who has married George Wilding, The Ddol. They have two sons, John and Gwynfor, and they are all living, and farming, at The Ddol.

Dorothy married Gerald Scott, a train driver, and moved to Shrewsbury. They have two sons, Robin and Graham, and both these boys have been good footballers. I have recently heard of them singing and conducting at their parents' diamond wedding anniversary, so music and football have carried on down the generations.

In the 1960s Ned and Irene gave up farming and they moved to Shrewsbury. Doug my husband, bought Brickhouse and farmed the land with The Waen, and we let the house to Ron and Anne Evans and their three children. They lived there for a few years, while Ron, who had bought Fiddlers Green, pulled the old house down and built a new bungalow there, and started a market garden, which had been his life's dream.

When they left, we ran it as a holiday cottage for a few years. Then, in 1978, David our son married Jackie Farmer and it became their first home for a few months. In December 1978, Doug and I and our family moved down to The Stores

Ned and Rene

Ned and Gwyneth and their two girls load muck on to the cart

and Post Office in the village, and David and Jackie moved to The Waen — where they still live today.

Brickhouse, or Bryn-mawr as it was now called, was then sold to Mr. and Mrs. Shaw and their daughter, Charlotte, who came to Beguildy School and was a very artistic little girl while she was in my class. The parents made many improvements to the house, and made a rather attractive fishpond up in the field. As Charlotte came of age to go to Presteigne School, they sold Brickhouse and moved to Knighton.

John and Sarah Sanford bought the property as a holiday home in December 1999. They then sold their house in Birmingham and moved out here permanently in October 2000. They run the five acres as a hobby smallholding, with sheep, hens and ducks. They also have a polytunnel, which enables them to grow their own fruit and vegetables. There are three pools now containing coarse fish, and these pools are mentioned, as a feature to look out for, in the guidebooks for Glyndwr's Way, which runs alongside their land.

From left to right: Graham, Gerald, Dorothy and Robert Scott

Down the Teme Valley

Friesland

This was a little *ty-un-nos* homestead, and is on the side of the main Knighton to Newtown road just below Bwlch-y-llyn. When it was first built in the early 18th century or even before, it would have been on open moorland, for then the road or track would have followed the river down the valley.

In the 1891 census an Edward Williams 51, and his wife Mary 38, lived there, but by 1901 it was recorded as 'Empty'. Later, we hear of a John Lewis and his wife Jane. He was a distant relative of mine, and was recorded living at Bwlch-y-llyn in 1901. Later, we hear of them living at Hafod Fadog before they set sail for Australia. The long sea journey must have kept them in the same place for several weeks. They lived in Australia for many years, then came back and bought three small farms in Stoke Prior near Leominster. They had no children, so Auntie Polly went down there to look after them, along with my sister, Hazel, then still in school, who went as company for her.

I think that Friesland may have been empty from then on. The Cwmgwyn Chapel people used it as their tearoom on Anniversary days and other special days, but now it is derelict and nearly down, but a beam above the fireplace has been taken out, and on it is carved the same initials as those found at the Prysg. Both these houses had a thatched roof, as possibly did many of these little houses when they were first built. The raw material for the thatch would be found locally, as would the stone for building the walls. Also, the floors were usually stone slabs laid directly on the soil, as we have heard about in some of the other homes. In those days, they had to make use of all the raw materials that were to hand.

There are still a couple of walls standing but the roof has all gone, so it will not be long before it will just be a memory.

The Gravel

This little cottage was in the valley below Cwmgwyn Chapel, and quite near the River Teme. In those days the road, such as it was, passed by the cottage, then on to Hafod Fadog and back up to where the road is today — joining near Cwmgwyn Hall.

In the 1901 census, John Lewis 50, his wife Sarah 39, Lavinia 13, and Pryce 11, lived there. This family had been living at Llethrau Cottage in 1891. John was a carpenter by trade and helped to build the extension to Cwmgwyn Chapel in 1908. He also used to repair clocks and watches.

I have been told that before the 1891 census a Mrs. Griffiths lived at The Gravel. She was a very thrifty, hardworking lady and some think she was the mother of the Rev. H.V. Griffiths, who owned The Ddol and Tyn-y-Cwm. She would take her basket of eggs and butter to sell in Newtown whatever the weather — and it was a walking ticket in those days. If it were very wet, she would wear a brown sack over her shoulders to keep out some of the rain. Men often used to wear these sacks over their shoulders to go out working on the farm in wet weather. They would be fastened with a bag-pin.

These brown sacks would have been brought to the farms full of animal cake or other such foodstuff for the animals. When emptied, they would be put to good use in many different ways. The farmer's wife would always have a bag apron, or rough apron, which she would wear to do the rough jobs outside, such as milking, feeding the pigs and poultry — jobs usually done by the women! Also, my mother would always wear her rough apron to 'send' our neighbour, an auntie for Betty Lloyd, Carreg-y-frain, and Vera Lakelin. Women often used to 'send' or walk with their friends and neighbours part of the way to their home. It would be a chance to have a nice talk without the rest of the family around, and my Mum would also use the opportunity to fill her rough apron with morning sticks, often enough for several days. If you wanted a cup of tea first thing in the morning, you made sure there were plenty of good dry sticks to burn and get the kettle boiling. Last year, when Tony Blackburn won the 'I'm a Celebrity — get me out of here', he was ridiculed for collecting all those sticks, but I think, as well as keeping a good fire day and night, he also kept himself sane.

Those brown sacks were also used as the base for the rag mats we used to make — often the only mats we ever had in the house. Then there would always be a bag at the outside door to get some of the mud off your boots — remember, wellies did not come into use until the 1930s. Also, there would be a roller towel made of sacking at the back door. This would get softer the more often it was washed.

Our flour for bread making was also brought in sacks, but these were white calico sacks, and again they were put to good use. I can remember making table-cloths, with drawn-thread work round the hems and embroidery in the centre, and also teacloths for drying the dishes, and here is a little true story. I have heard about a lady who, while cycling home from an Anniversary, fell off her bike and landed in the ditch with her skirt up around her head, and there — plain for all to see was written: SPILLERS SELF-RAISING FLOUR. Ouch! A bit itchy and hard. But I have wandered away from The Gravel.

John Lewis, The Gravel, was my Auntie Polly's uncle and, of course, my dad's uncle too, but she was the eldest of a family of eleven, and he was next to the youngest, so did not know — or was not interested in — what was going on before his time.

She used to tell me of her journeys from Abbey-cwm hir to Felindre, which means 'mill town'. She travelled pony-back and would bring fleeces of sheep's wool over to the mill in Felindre, which was about where the bottom of our garden is now. The field alongside is called Rack Meadow, which is where the fleece, after it had been washed, was hung out to dry. Then she would go to The Stores — it was never called 'the Shop' — and upstairs to a large room above it, where there would be two tailors sitting cross-legged on the floor, and eight or nine seamstresses working on garments for people. She would then be measured for a suit or what-ever garment she wanted making, and she would have to return three or four weeks later to pay and collect.

'Meredith Thomas and Sons' from Knighton, who built The Stores in 1877, had several children, and his youngest son came to visit us just after we moved down here in 1978. He was quite an elderly man and wanted to see his 'old home'. He told me that if someone important had died in Felindre, and several 'funeral black' were needed in a hurry, then some of his workers from his shop in Knighton would come up and help in the room above the Stores. How I wish now that I had asked him more about his life in Felindre way back when he lived here.

On her way back home, Auntie Polly would stop at The Gravel to have a cup of tea and a chat with her uncle. I think that this Lewis family were the last to live at The Gravel. John Lewis, the father, who was several years older than Sarah his wife, died — but I have not been able to find out when he died or where he is buried. It is not in Beguildy Church or Felindre Baptist Chapel yard. Pryce Lewis and his mother ended their days at the Coach House in Beguildy. Sarah died in 1937 aged 75, and Pryce died in 1952 aged 62. Both are buried in Felindre Chapel yard. Lavinia, their daughter and her husband Edward Lewis, who lived at Stapleton, Presteigne, are also buried in Felindre near to their parents.

There is little trace of The Gravel today — just a few stones and a memory.

Hafod Fadog

This is another little cottage on the banks of the River Teme, just lower down the valley than The Gravel, but unlike The Gravel this house has been lived in nearly all through the century, and is still occupied today.

In the 1901 census we find a James Evans 45, his wife Jane also 45, and their children Mary 14, Margaret 12, John 10, and Edith 6, together with Elizabeth Lewis 20, a stepdaughter. I know no more about this family although I have read about a James Evans and his wife Jane living at either The Gorther or The Gorther Mill, and also a Rev. James Evans from Medwaledd who became the vicar of Kerry.

Later, we hear about a great-uncle of mine, who had lived at Bwlch-y-llyn in 1901, then moved to Friesland, then on to Hafod Fadog. This was John Lewis and his wife Jane, originally from Abbey-cwm-hir. People in those days seemed to move quite often. These little houses were small and all about the same shape and size, so it was just a case of choosing a fine day, draw the horse and cart up outside the door, and load on their furniture and possessions, which would not be many, and away to go. Simple, wasn't it? — especially thinking about it nearly a hundred years later! Moving today is a traumatic experience for most of us. I have heard about one lady in this area moving forty times in as many years, but she left each house beautifully decorated and spotlessly clean. I wish she had been around when I was moving!

John and Jane Lewis duly moved again, but this time they set sail for Australia, a that journey kept them quiet for a few weeks. They stayed over there for many years, then returned with enough money to buy three smallholdings in Stoke Prior, Leominster.

The next family to live at Hafod Fadog were Charles Stephens and Una Wilding, The Ddol. They had started their married life at Cwmgwyn Hall. Charles was a son for Cwmgwyn Hall, and when his brother, John, married Ella Wilding, a sister for Una, they all lived at the Hall for a time. Then Charles and Una, and two of their children, Martin and Olwen, moved to Hafod Fadog, and their eldest son, Burton, stayed at the Hall, and remained there until he died in 1994 at the age of 78, and is buried in Felindre Baptist Chapel yard.

Una and Charles were very good supporters of Cwmgwyn Chapel, as were their children, Martin and Olwen. Martin and his dad were very good bass singers and were always in the choir. I can remember that at the practices for the Anniversary, when we had agreed on which pieces to sing, Charlie would always say — 'And what about *The Lily of the Valley*?' but I don't ever remember singing it at Cwmgwyn.

Olwen would always bring a large dish full of home-made butter to spread on the home-made bread for the Anniversary tea, which would be a plate of bread and butter, cheese, jam, Welsh cakes, a slab of Scribona's fruit cake and one slab of their 'plain' — no ready made sandwiches in those days. A few days before the Anniversary both Ella and Una would be up in the chapel on their hands and knees scrubbing the wooden floor. I once offered to help — but that was their job. They were both wonderful workers for the chapel. During the wartime they had two little brothers evacuated there and Una loved these little boys, and they loved living at Hafod Fadog.

Charlie died in 1962 aged 79, and Una died in 1972 aged 89, and they are both buried in Felindre. Martin and Olwen continued to live at Hafod Fadog, although Olwen was away working for most of the week. They had quite a lot of work done on the house and the big job was to raise the roof, making it a higher house. In 1980 Martin died a few days before the Anniversary. He was 64 years old, and Olwen tragically died in a car crash in 1987 aged 67. Both are buried in Felindre Baptist yard. I think Hafod Fadog was then left empty for a few years.

Today Mair and John Stephens live there. Mair is a daughter for Frances and David Morris, Pound Gate, who regularly attend Cwmgwyn, and are both in the choir, and John is the fifth John Stephens of Cwmgwyn Hall. John is also our main organist, and has also helped Bryan McCann with a lot of the work in the chapel.

In 2004 we had the good news that Mair and John are now the proud parents of a little son (see the photograph).

John and Mair Stephens and their son

Cwmgwyn Hall

This is a very old farmhouse, and the Stephens family have farmed there for many years. The first Stephens of whom we have knowledge is Elizabeth Stephens who was buried in Beguildy Church yard in 1812. She had two sons — Evan and Edward. Evan was christened on Christmas Day in Beguildy Church 1785. He married Sarah Edwards and they moved down to South Wales, most probably to work in the coalmines.

Their first son, John Stephens, was born in Tredegar in 1815, and also three other children, then they moved back up to this area, and their last five children were born at The Llethrau. This John Stephens married a Rachael and they moved into Cwmgwyn Hall, so becoming the first John Stephens at Cwmgwyn Hall. They are both buried in Llanbadarn Church yard, so possibly Rachael was a Llanbadarn girl. They had three children, and their first son, another John, was the second John Stephens at Cwmgwyn Hall.

This John Stephens married Jane Elizabeth Brown from The Hendy, said to be related to Austin Richards and also to Mary Morris, who was Mary Brown before she married. They married in 1873, and both are buried in Beguildy Church yard, Jane in 1900 and John in 1919. They had four children — John Llewelyn, George, Charles and Sarah, John Llewelyn Stephens being the third John Stephens at Cwmgwyn Hall. He was born in 1876 and in 1915 married Ella Wilding from The Ddol, and they lived at Cwmgwyn Hall together with Charles, John's brother, and Una Wilding, Ella's sister, whom Charles had married some years before. Later Charles and Una moved to Hafod Fadog with their two younger children, Olwen and Martin, but their first son, Burton, remained at the Hall until he died in 1994, and is buried in Felindre Baptist Chapel yard.

Margaret Stephens just about to shake hands with Prince Charles. Joan (the Garn) is also there and later the ladies sang 'We'll keep a welcome' to the prince

George lived at the Hendy and married Jane Lewis, Rhos-goch (near the Rhuvid) and Sarah married Evan Lloyd, Great Rhuvid, and later they emigrated to Canada.

John Llewelyn and Ella had two children — another John Llewelyn and Mary Jane. This John Stephens is the 'John the Hall' as many of us knew him, and is the fourth John Stephens at Cwmgwyn Hall. His sister, Mary Jane, sadly died young in 1949 at the age of 33, and is buried with her parents in Felindre Baptist yard — John, their father, was buried in 1937, and Ella in 1965.

Margaret with her family: Mair Thomas and John Stephens on their wedding day May 2001. The photograph was taken by Dolfrynog fishpool

John the Hall and Burton continued to live at Cwmgwyn Hall after Ella's death. Then in 1975, John married Margaret Savage from Llanfair Caereinion. Margaret was a Sister in Newtown Hospital and great friends with Ruby Davies, who used to live at The Waen, and they both came out to Cwmgwyn Chapel some Sundays.

John and Margaret have three children — Alwena, John Erfyl, and Ruth, so there was yet another John Stephens at Cwmgwyn Hall, although he is now married and lives at Hafod Fadog with his wife Mair. Alwena is also married and lives at the Prysg with Charles Campbell, her husband, and Ruth works in Shrewsbury, at the moment, but has worked and trained in Cardiff.

This Stephens family are all very musical, as I'm sure were all the Stephens families before, and they have all been, and still are, very faithful to Cwmgwyn Chapel. Sadly, John the Hall died in 1997 aged 76, but his love of Cwmgwyn Chapel and music still live on in his wife and children.

Tynllidiart

This was another of our little dwellings which have nearly all disappeared. It was just at the top of the Hendy pitch on the right hand side, going up. Apart from a few stones, there is a gate going into a field off the road, which is still called Tynllidiart gate.

Back in the mid-19th century, a Mr. and Mrs. Griffiths lived there with their children, but they emigrated to Canada. Then in the 1891 census a William Hughes, aged 50 and a farmer, his wife Mary 43, and their children, Arthur 10, Albert 7, and Jessie 5, lived there, and also Edward and Thomas Lloyd, stepsons.

Last year one of my sons, Graham, had been called out to a firm somewhere in the Midlands. Having repaired the machine, he was just about to leave when the boss came out, and in the conversation asked Graham how far he had to travel to get home. Graham, who was staying with me at that time, replied, 'Just over the border into Wales'. The boss then said he used to visit his grandparents years ago, and they lived just over the border in a little village called Felindre. What a coincidence! His grandparents were William and Mary Hughes and his father was Arthur. He remembered that it was a thatched cottage in those days. What a small world we live in!

In the 1901 census we find William and Mary, with their daughter Jessie, who by then was 15, all living at Cork Hall, which is just across the road, but no mention of the boys. They had most probably gone out to work, and Arthur possibly went to the Midlands to find work.

One day in 2004, four folk were strolling through the village and glancing from side to side as if looking for something. Austin Richards was just leaving the shop, so they went up to talk with him — they wanted to know where was Tynllidiart, as the one lady's father was Albert Hughes. She could remember, as a young girl, going to Hope's Castle to visit. Austin had a long chat with them and I'm sure he could remember lots of the history of Tynllidiart and the homes around to tell them.

I think that the Hughes family were the last family to live at Tynllidiart.

Little House

In the 1891 census we find a John Mantle 54, his wife, Mary 73, their daughter, Mary 35, and grandsons, John 21, Edwin 12 and Phillip 7. Then by 1901 only John 64, and his grandson, Phillip 17, were there. Mary, his wife had died in 1899. John and Phillip moved to Cork Hall where John died, aged 82. He and his wife are buried in Beguildy Church yard.

Then Reuben Morgan from Fiddlers Green bought Little House, and he and his sister, Jane, farmed there for several years. These two were children of Naomi and Richard Morgan of Fiddlers Green, and both were never married.

Later, we hear of Mr. John (Jack) Mills, (a son for Mariah Mills, née Morgan. of Fiddlers Green), and his wife Myfanwy, who was a great granddaughter for Naomi and a granddaughter for Jane, who was already living at Little House. Jane, although never married, had had a daughter, Kate, who was brought up with her granny, Naomi, at Fiddlers Green. Kate then married a Jones, and Myfanwy and her sister, Daisy Davies from Hall of the Forest, were two of their children. Thus John and Myfanwy moved into Little House with their older relations.

Mr and Mrs. Mills had their first three children, Reuben, Glenys and Mary, while at Little House. All these folk were loyal supporters of Cwmgwyn Chapel and in 1942 John Mills was appointed as a trustee. Reuben had been a trustee since the very early days of the chapel as a Baptist. Myfanwy had a very good voice and was also a good organist. She could just play by ear and changed into different keys to suit the singers, but she could also read music. It is amazing how music carries down through the generations — especially before the days of the telly!

Later that year the Mills family moved to The Llethrau with Reuben and Mary, but left Glenys with the older relations, Reuben and Jane Morgan, at Little House. They stayed there and farmed the land until it was sold to the Craddock family in 1946. They then moved to Medwaledd where Jack and Myfanwy were then living.

Memories of Little House *by* Effie Haynes (Craddock)

My parents paid £900 for Little House in 1946. I was then only eighteen months old. My dad was 41 and mum 42. We bought the farm from Mr. Reuben Morgan, senior. He lived with his nephew and granddaughter in Little House, which comprised two rooms downstairs and two small bedrooms adjoining each other. After they moved, Mr. Jack Mills, junior, used to come for well water for his uncle, who by this time was almost blind. They had moved to a larger house and farm at Medwaledd, near Felindre.

The day we moved, mum and I came on the bus from Knighton, which terminated at Felindre, two miles from Little House. Mum was loaded with bags, yet all I kept saying was 'Carry me, Mum'. My mum said, 'You will have to walk. I can't carry you — I have all these bags.' My dad was on his way with Kitty, the pony, again loaded, but we all made it to Little House. It must have taken him a while to cover the fifteen miles from Stapleton, where we then lived.

Little House was $62\frac{1}{2}$ acres of land and mum and dad farmed this with our horse, Dolly, carts, horse cutters, ploughs, etc. During the war, the Ministry of Defence, locally called 'the War Agr.' ploughed the hill ground up for potatoes. We kept cows, sheep and a pig for our own use. I used to disappear when the pig was killed, and said I would never marry a farmer, and I never did.

Mum and dad with our two sheepdogs

Mum was the 'cowman', having lived at The Mill, Norton, with her brother before marrying dad. Her brother was the miller, and she milked the cows and took the milk round the village each day. At weekends, she made bread and churned the butter for her customers. Mum continued to make butter at Little House, which my father loved. To the disgust of dad, I preferred shop butter. Dad was the shepherd and loved his sheep. He mainly kept Cluns. I watched him draw lambs, and very often he would go for George, the Hendy, or Bill Barnett to help if it was a difficult birth. Maybe this was the reason I ended being a midwife.

Thinking back to mum and her cows — there was a spate of the often fatal Hereford disease in the area, and we had one cow go down with it. The vet came and did the necessary, and mum, dad and George, the Hendy, put up a tent over the cow and mum kept giving her gruel, as well as what the vet had prescribed. They got her up on her feet and put bales of straw around her to keep her up. Eventually she got better and one day produced a calf. The vet called by one day later and said he couldn't understand why this cow had lived and most of the others around had died. I put it down to the 'nurse' in my mother — she was always looking after someone.

Mum with the beloved cattle

Mr. and Mrs. Lloyd were the neighbours above us at Crochen. Mum would pick up our bread from out on the main road every Thursday afternoon, Mr. Watts having delivered it in a van from J.O. Davies, Llandrindod Wells. This would last a week. In school holidays I would go up with mum, but sometimes we would have to wait an hour or even longer in the winter for the van to arrive. We would carry our bread home, then go back for the Lloyd's bread and carry

Effie, the carthorse and dad. Look at the rough field

that to Crochen. We would have a cup of tea, exchange all the news and mum would do some housework for them. Mr. Lloyd would tell me some riddles, and laugh heartily while I tried to solve them. They certainly were characters. They had some lovely ornaments including a pair of white dogs with gold chains, and also some other expensive looking items. This must have fired my love of antiques.

Mum did all her cooking in a pot on the open fire until one year she sold all her blackcurrants and raspberries in Newtown, and bought a Valor paraffin stove with the money. It was wonderful to have a roast dinner on a Sunday for the first time in my life, and I would then be about ten years old.

I started at Beguildy School at the age of five when Mr. and Mrs. Jones were the teachers. My transport was from the main road with Mr. Rogers, Gwernerrin, and his old black taxi. One day he shut the door with my little finger in the hinge. I was too frightened to say anything as I was so painfully shy, but I still have the scar to this day.

Mrs. Jones was very strict, especially if you didn't get your tables right first time. Once she was very cross with me, and pulled my knickers down in front of the class and tanned my backside. I was so embarrassed in front of the boys and too ashamed to tell my parents. It was years later I told my mum. She always made lovely toffee for the school party and said, had she known, that there would have been no more toffee. Another day, I missed the school car, and mum sent me with the postman in his van, with me hiding in the back. I must have arrived mid-morning and went into the porch to hear Mrs. Jones thrashing one of the pupils. With that, I turned round and walked the four miles back home. Mum asked me why I was home so early and I told her it would have been my turn next for a thrashing for being late.

But it was not all bad in school. We had Welsh lessons, percussion, weaving (a scarf, I still have it) and embroidery. In the summer, we went out into their garden and drew pictures or played with Plasticine, which I loved. I could daydream or listen to the birds or look at the lovely orange poppies with their black centres, which I still love. Mr. Jones in top class was more easy-going, and liked me. I was more confident in his class. One day, I went to the toilet and left the class door open. He shouted, 'Spring doors at Little House, are there?' I looked at him a bit blank for a while, then went red and cottoned on to what he meant. Every Friday afternoon he would read us a story — so many chapters every week. *Wind in the Willows* was one I remember with fondness. Mr. Jones suffered from asthma, and would suck his cough sweets all the way through the lessons and would only stop to pop another sweet into his mouth.

The year we left, Mr. and Mrs. Jones retired. My classmates and I carried the books over to the new school. The teachers were young and very enthusiastic, but we only spent a few months with them before moving on to secondary school. I stood next to my then little boyfriend, Johnny Beavan, and Mr. Gibson-Watt opened the new school. It was a lovely modern school with more classrooms and several teachers. Joyce Roberts, The Travelly, was my best friend, and she would sometimes come and have tea with me. Fifty years later, we are still friends and we now live in the same village.

When I was five, my father bought me a donkey from Elvert Beavan — John's father. The donkey was called Neddy and I loved him. My cousins used to come up from the south and they loved to ride Neddy. One year when I was 'Potato Queen', Neddy was harnessed up to go in the cart. My dad was quite artistic with the plaques, and we would have had first prize at Felindre Sports, so he said, only Neddy's back feet had not been cut. Dad would cut the front feet, but Neddy wouldn't stay still to have the back ones cut, so dad used to take him to Pryce Brick, the blacksmith, and even Pryce used to swear at Neddy!

Neddy the donkey giving rides to Effie's cousins

It was a sad day for me when Neddy went back to John Beavan's. I had outgrown him and because he was not ridden enough he became playful and frisky and started to chase the sheep, so he had to go.

I then started riding the carthorses, Dolly and Blackie, which frightened my mum to death. My dad never had a tractor, so all the farm work was done by horses. He was an accomplished horseman, and had the fox's tail and stirrups for being first at the fox's kill. This was something I hated the thought of, and in later years I couldn't even kill a hen!

My dad would put me on a horse to break it in. I remember Mr. Bill Barnett, The Rhuvid, saying, 'That child will get killed' but my father said, 'She will be O.K.' He never saw danger. My mum was much more nervous and preferred her cycle to horses.

I hated school and looked forward to school holidays, although I always had to work on the farm. My sheepdog and I would collect all the sheep off the hill to be dipped in Felindre, in Bright's dipping bath. Then there was the harvest. The summers always seemed hotter in our happy memories of childhood. Dad would cut all round the whole field with old Isaac, the scythe, and sometimes he would cut down the whole field. Other times he would help George Stephens for a day, and George would cut a field or two for us. Mum and I would cock the hay, after it have been turned and dried with the carthorse and tedder. Then mum and I would tread the load down on the dray, while Dad pitched it up to us, and the same in the granary. On our stony fold, riding in the dray back to the field, we would be

Little House — a typical farmyard in the 1950s

jogging along when once a pikel stuck in my forehead drawing blood, but not too serious. Sometimes mum would fill a bottle with cider and put it under the hedge to keep cool, and sometimes as a special treat we would have cheese and onion sandwiches. But in the evening we always had to be home by a quarter to seven to listen to the Archers. Little did I think that my daughter would be married to Shula Archer's son, Barney.

Looking back, my childhood was idyllic, although we struggled financially, but that was made up with love. My parents doted on me, being an only child and conceived late in life. We never had much money and mum said that it was often difficult to find the dinner money on a Monday morning for me to take to school. Mum used to skin moles and nail the skin to a board to dry, after which she would sell them for cash. Moleskin waistcoats for men were very popular at that time.

Mr. Nicholls, Llanddewi, would come every week to collect our eggs — all washed and put in wooden boxes. He would give us the cash right away, and then he would have a cup of tea and write out next week's order for our groceries. When we sold some stock, he would be paid. My parents would say how trusting they were to pay us the egg money when we still owed them for our groceries.

When I had some spare time from helping on the farm and doing the washing up, which mum hated, I would play in the stream running down by the side of the fold. I would spend hours damming up the water to make a pool, and then sailing my boats, which my dad's family had given me. My mum would send dad's relations eggs and a dressed chicken in a tin box and in return, they would fill the box with hand-down clothes and goodies. I remember once having a lovely Scots kilt with a pin in it from my cousin in Scotland. Mrs. Jones from Beguildy School said that I should keep that for my grandchildren, but it was eventually passed on to a neighbour's children.

Church or Chapel on a Sunday were very much part of my life. I went with dad to Crug-y-Byddar Church and to Cwmgwyn with mum. Aggie Stephens from the

Our eggs were collected from the farm — or the main road, and taken to Llandewi where there was the nearest egg-packing station. There they were graded and packed, then taken to sell in the big towns and cities

Hendy was a lovely lady and would often walk with us to Church on a Sunday. Mum would clean the church on Saturday and light the old black stove on Sunday. I helped with the cleaning. Mum loved brass and there was a square black safe/box near the altar, and I remember mum once saying to me, 'Let's try and clean this up'. Each week we would rub a little more and eventually it shone like gold. My dad was sidesman and rang the bells. Canon Jones was the vicar and he used to arrive in his blue Morris 1000 car. On snowy days, it would be only my dad and me and the vicar there.

Cwmgwyn Chapel was a great favourite with me. I used to walk up to the Hall and then have a lift with Mr. John Stephens, the conductor and organist. The last Sunday in June was the Anniversary. There was a service at 2 pm and at 6 pm with a tea in between. We were practising the choir pieces for several weeks before, and I had two recitations to learn — one for afternoon and one for evening. The young lads would be outside, throwing small stones up on the roof to roll down, making a big noise inside the chapel.

With the Anniversary, came the bluebells in our own bluebell wood. Philip Vallance bought the whole field with the wood in, so that it would not be ploughed up and the bluebells lost.

I remember my dad shearing in the back kitchen at Little House. The furniture would be pushed back, and they sheared the sheep on the flagstones. Dad would shear while mum turned the handle. Mum would scrub the flagstones each night. Once the shearing was finished, the wool would be wrapped and packed into a huge sack, which mum would sew across the top and it would be ready for Passey Nott to collect.

I also remember being in hospital three times while living at Little House. The last time was very serious. Dr. Garman was called out — Dad, having gone down to the Bricks, our neighbours, at Cefnbedw to phone. The doctor diagnosed osteomyelitis and announced, 'Hospital, at once — or she will be dead in forty-eight hours', but he saved my life and I will be ever grateful to Dr. Garman. Later, I went in for nursing as I had always wanted, and became a midwife in Knighton hospital, having trained in Cheltenham.

My parents moved back to Norton in 1963, to look after my auntie who was wheelchair-bound, and Little House was eventually sold to Mr. Philip Vallance in 1972. It is still called Little House, but it is now a very big fine house, and has had a lot of money spent on it.

Philip has also written his own account of life at Little House:

I bought Little House in 1972. I was a young barrister, living in London but practising mainly on the old Oxford circuit, and wanted somewhere to stay while working in the old Assize towns of Shrewsbury, Hereford, Gloucester and Worcester. I also had always wanted a weekend/holiday home in mid-Wales.

I eventually found Little House. It had not been lived in for some years and was in a very run-down condition. It had been bought (presumably from Sam

Little House as it is today — with the same name, but more like a mansion

Wendy accepts the flowers from Samantha George. Philip, Rev. Stuart Dobson and Mr. John Peregrine look on

Craddock or his estate) by Reid-Macintosh Associates, a two-man firm who were trying to make money by buying up small Welsh farms, selling off most of the land and then renovating the farmhouse to sell to people like me. They had already sold off the land (to John Roberts) and had secured a priced quote for the renovation from Bill Preece of Knighton, to a design by F.T. Moore (also of Knighton). They were in financial difficulties because of the then oil crisis, and so I was able to persuade them to sell me the house, plus the building contract, together with the fields immediately around the house (some six acres).

The building work was completed by May 1973, and I took up occupation. In June 1973, I married Wendy. We have spent most of our holidays etc. at Little House, and our children — Henry 24, and Lucy 23, have grown to love the place, especially Henry.

In about 1980, David Barrett built a stone porch outside the lower front door, and in about 1995, he built a new wing, also out of stone, on the north end of the house. This has made the house much more extensive and comfortable. He was helped in this project by his brother-in-law, David Smith. More recently, David's brother Christopher (Bono) has taken over the role of builder / carpenter / handyman and, in particular, has successfully undertaken the installation of water storage tanks to increase our reservoir capacity (of water from the spring up the hill) to some 3,000 gallons.

In the early years, the work of hedging and fencing around the perimeter of the fields was undertaken by Frank Richards, the Lane House. Since about 1992, this has been done by Morris Thomas from Newtown. He also mows the garden.

Apart from keeping it structurally sound, I have done nothing to the stone barn below the house, with the consequence that the barn is now one of the last of its sort in the valley, most of the others having been pulled down and replaced by steel structures to meet the requirements of modern farming.

What we call 'the Bluebell Wood' was part of the land bought by John Roberts. In about 1985, I discovered he was preparing to loose sheep into it and, no doubt, plough and re-seed it. Luckily, I was able to persuade him to sell it to me (some two acres). I have fenced it off and, apart from planting some (native) trees, have left it as it is — my own legacy to the next generation.

The Bluebell Wood

Thank you, Philip — but I must have the last word!

Wendy and Phillip come out to Little House often, and are always willing and ready to support local events in the area. In 1997, Philip, in his capacity as a barrister, witnessed the signing in of the new trustees at Cwmgwyn Chapel. They will also come out from London to attend a funeral of a local person, whom they knew well.

Both Wendy and Philip officially opened our 'new' Village Hall. We had a grant to help repair and extend our hall, which was originally built in 1950 and was re-opened in 2000.

Their children, Henry and Lucy, also enjoy coming out to Little House with some of their friends but, of course, they are not children anymore.

Holdings with a turn-out on to Cwmgwyn hills

Butterwell

This is another little dwelling on the edge of the Crown land, and by its size and situation would have been a little *ty-un-nos*. It is said that the very cool water in the well gave it the name of Butterwell, as butter needed to be kept very cool while making. Also, farmers' wives from the Llanbadarn and Llanbister areas, on their way to Newtown market, would sit and rest on the roadside by Butterwell, and if it was a very hot day they would lower their basket of butter down into the well to cool it before setting out on the second part of their journey to Newtown.

In addition, in the 12th century, it was said to be holy water, so perhaps St. David, in his travels across Wales many years before, had stopped there to drink its water. St. David had already visited Abbey-cwm-hir, and had stopped to drink at the well just above the Llaithddu — now called David's Well.

The first person we find living at Butterwell in 1901 was a Mary Davies. She was a widow who had come from the Abbey-cwm-hir area. Although she was a lame

> IN AFFECTIONATE REMEMBRANCE OF
> ## MARY DAVIES,
> The beloved wife of Richard Davies, of Butterwell, Llanbadarn-fynydd.
>
> *Who fell asleep January 23rd. 1924*
> IN HER 65TH YEAR.
> Interred at Maesyrhelem Burial Ground January 28th.
>
> ❀ ❀ ❀
>
> I go to life, and not to death,
>   From darkness to life's native sky;
> I go from sickness and from pain
>   To health and immortality.

woman, she used to walk to Cwmgwyn Chapel every Sunday, using her umbrella as a walking stick. I have heard people say that they always knew when she entered the chapel because it would be 'step-bang, step-bang', as she walked up to her seat.

The next couple we hear about are Bessie and Fred Davies from Dolfrynog. Butterwell was their first home after they were married, then later they moved to Upper Green, Llanbadarn, and then to Cwmcorn, Dolfor. Ruth Morgan is one of their daughters, and she has written to me with information about her parents and also the Davies family, Dolfrynog. Bessie and Fred had another daughter, Margaret, and also I have heard of two sons — one was Bill, who was a keen footballer in his youth.

Maggie Pugh lived here at one time, but she did not stay in any place for long. She was unmarried, and there was an unmarried woman living in most areas; where I lived, we had Patty Evans who would come to help once or twice a year. She would stay with us for about a week, and would always make a new dress for us three girls, ready for the Anniversary. We used to dread her coming because she would comb our hair from underneath, and boy, did we squeal!

Butterwell seems to have been quite an important place in the early 20th century, and most probably before. At that time, this road was the main road from

Butterwell, with Lynne Jones, their son Tom and their two springer spaniels

Llandrindod Wells to Newtown, and was called 'the one horse road'. This was because when it was built it did not go 'over' any hills but around them, and whilst it made the road longer with more bends in, it meant that a loaded cart could get to Newtown with only one horse. On fine days, especially Tuesdays — Newtown Fair days — the whole town would be like a street market, with the people living around setting up their stalls, and trying to sell their wares. Life was hard for these people living in their little homes on the hills, so they needed to make money by whatever means they could. In the census forms, there is one column for 'occupation' and we read of knitters, dressmakers, stocking makers, shoe and clog makers, basket and wisket makers, candle makers, tailors and quilters. All these occupations could be carried out in the home, and much of the raw material needed was found locally and made use of. Sheep's wool for knitters, rushes for candles, parts of different trees for baskets and clogs, and wood for carts and furniture and, of course, stones and wood for making homes.

My grandmother and mother were Welsh quilters, and I was taught how to make a sheep's wool quilt while I was still in primary school. I have made several quilts since, and even about eight years ago, my sister Hazel and I made one as a wedding present to send over to New Zealand. Anne Harries, Pantycaragle, had been helping to shear the sheep at her home just before her wedding and I, with her brother Edward's help, had smuggled out one of the fleeces that Anne had actually shorn, and we used it in the quilt.

Knitting was an ongoing occupation for both men and women, and as it was all pure wool — no nylon or other man-made fibres to reinforce the toes and heels, and as many men wore socks up to their knees, holes would be darned several times, then they would be re-footed. Mrs. Phoebe Reynolds, who is 92 years old, still knits socks for her son, and re-foots them when needed. Jumpers and shawls

The centre of this quilt was going to be aeroplanes passing between New Zealand and Britain, but my eye-sight failed me

Bill (Buckle) Price

would also be made of pure wool — and oh! those itchy vests. What a wonderful invention was the liberty bodice!

Knitting could also be carried on wherever you were. We read of some women who would keep knitting while walking to Newtown to sell their butter and eggs, and bring a few groceries home with them. Charlie, who lived in a little house by Windy Hall, used to sit up in the quarry by Butterwell and knit all day. Later, Richard Davies lived at Charlie's, and he would also sit up in the quarry and knit. The quarry became known as 'Dickie's Chair'.

Of course, knitting and most of the other crafts could be carried on in the wintertime, when the nights were long. Candles or oil lamps were used for light, and usually one candle per room would give enough light for the whole family to keep working. It amuses me when we have a power cut these days, my son and his young family have to have at least a dozen candles around the room — I still manage with one!! Some things are hard to change.

Lynne Jones, the present owner, has written to me with a little more up-to-date information. A William Price and his wife, Jenny, lived there just after the war. Jenny used to work at Penithon Hall for the Haig (whisky) family. Also working there were Jane Easson (John Davies, Bwlch-y-llyn's mother) and Mrs. Hughes (Phoebe Reynolds' mother) and several other maids and housekeepers. It sounds as if these young girls had a good time working for the gentry, and especially the Haigs. The families living on the estate would also be given lavish parties at the 'big house' with music, dancing and games for all, and especially at Christmas-time there would be a very big Christmas tree with presents for all the children on the estate.

William Pryce died in 1950 and is buried in Llananno Church yard, but I can find out very little about Jenny, only that she remained very good friends with Jane Davies, Bwlch-y-llyn. Butterwell then remained empty for a few years, until the Council were supposed to have re-housed a family there in about 1963. After this family left, a tree blew down and fell on the roof at the back.

Then a photographer, Mr. John Nesbitt, wanted to buy Butterwell from Mr. John Davies, Bwlch-y-llyn, who now owned the dwelling, but John Davies was not keen to sell until John Nesbitt said he knew Jenny Price, whereupon the sale went ahead. Had he not bought it and restored it, Butterwell could well have declined into just a heap of stones and a memory.

In 1980 Chris and Lynne bought Butterwell from John Nesbitt. They had stopped at The Stores to ask Doug the way, and also wanted to borrow a roasting tin to cook their lamb dinner in the Rayburn. Lynne is a Member of Parliament in the Midlands and we often see and hear her on the television, and Chris is a scientist. Since then, they have worked hard improving their holiday home. Lynne says that when they first went out there, the worms used to come up through the cracks between the stone slabs. At Butterwell, their main project in 2003 was to take up all the stone floors, put a damp-course in, and then lay Welsh floor tiles. In 1986, Chris set up a windmill to generate electricity. This provides lights for the house, and also with the help of storage batteries and other complicated electrical equations, it pumps the water from that cold well into the house. Lynne and Chris have two sons, and when they were younger, they used to bring their bikes out to ride on the quiet roads by Butterwell, and also their Springer spaniels used to enjoy the open hills to run wild and free.

Chris has set up a windmill to generate electricity

And so yet another of our little homesteads has been saved, and we hope will be enjoyed for a few more years.

Lower Voil, Blaen-Voil and Blaen-cwm-Voil

Originally, I think, all these three homesteads would have been built as our little *ty-un-nos* houses, as they are a long way out across the open hill between Butterwell and the Llaithddu turn, but to my surprise they are all in Beguildy Parish. I have always heard that this parish was a long, narrow stretch of land, but to extend from nearly in Knighton right over to the Llaithddu bridge is a long way. Also, I have heard that years ago at harvest time, it was one of the duties of the vicar to travel round the perimeter of his parish. Well, it's fortunate that in those days most people enjoyed pony-trekking — even the vicar.

In the 1880s Lower Voil was bought by a Mr. Lees from Cheshire, who by trade was a coach-maker. He and his family used to come out to Llanbadarn for holidays

Lower Voil (or, as the new owner now spells it, Lower Foel) covered in ivy

and it seems that he decided to rebuild the house, (just as many other little homesteads were being rebuilt around that time), at the same time extending it and making it more elaborate inside. Perhaps this Mr. Lees himself was the builder, or at least the carpenter, as the windows and staircase had some lovely carved wood — still plain to see, for, considering his trade, he would have known how to work with wood.

I do not know if the Lees family ever lived there. In the 1891 census we read of a Mrs. Bliss 51, and her two daughters Mary 9, and Emily 8, and Mary Jones 20, John Davies 16, and John Morgan 25, all living there, the last two lads being servants. Emrys Jones, who later lived at Lower Voil, remembers the initials E.B. and M.B. carved on a beam in the shed and also on some trees around. This was something that was often done in those days, and has proved to be very interesting and, sometimes, useful a hundred or so years later. Even I can remember carving my initials on a beam in the barn, but it took me several evenings to finish it.

By the 1901 census, the Bliss family have left and a Thomas Rowlands 61, and his wife Sarah 65, were living there, but I know no more about this couple. I am amazed that an elderly couple would want to move to such a remote place, but perhaps in those days they had to walk long distances and so kept themselves fit.

The next family we hear about living at Lower Voil were the Evans family — now living at The Upper Llaithddu Farm. Trevor was born in 1916 at Lower Voil, and went to the Llaithddu School and to Penithon Chapel. On special days, he would walk to Cwmgwyn Chapel. He also remembers walking their sheep over to The Wain to be put through the dipping bath. This was a long, narrow bath filled with water and a very strong-smelling disinfectant mixed in. The sheep had to swim slowly through this, and so allow the disinfectant to get right down through the wool to their skin. This was to stop the flies laying their eggs on the sheep, and when the eggs hatched into maggots, they would feed on the sheep and could sometimes cause death. (Dipping for sheep scab was only introduced in the 1960s.)

The Evans family left Lower Voil in 1929, and moved first to the Camnant, then to the Upper Llaithddu Farm, where Trevor and his brother, Stanley, still live. Trevor is a good singer, and still sings in the Newtown Male Voice Choir. He had two sisters who were also very musical as, of course, were his parents and grandparents before him. I have heard from my father years ago that there was a hymn tune attributed to the Evans family, but I do not know which hymn.

The next family to live at Lower Voil were Rhys Jones and his wife Elsie and their two children, Brenda and Emrys, who went to the Llaithddu School. When the war started they were issued with ration books and as Lower Voil is in Beguildy parish, their ration books said they had to collect their rations from Beguildy

Trevor Evans, who was born at Lower Voil in 1916, with Margaret Lewis and Bill (the Garn)

Noel Pugh, Megan Savage, Layton Pugh, Brenda Jones, Linda Powell and Emrys Jones. Emrys and Brenda lived at Lower Voil, the Pugh brothers at Bryn-Bedwyn. This picture shows Layton and Brenda at their wedding in Penithon Chapel in 1947

Shop. Brenda, being the oldest, had to take their books to school and ask the headmaster, Mr. Sibley, if he could have them changed to the Llaithddu Shop, and thankfully, they were all changed. The trip to Beguildy would have been a good ten miles or more.

Again, this family all attended Penithon Chapel, and Emrys became their organist when he was older. While living at Lower Voil, Brenda got married in Penithon Chapel and Megan Savage, who is now a regular attendee at Cwmgwyn Chapel, was her bridesmaid. Emrys and his wife have now retired and live near Llandrindod Wells, but he still comes back to Penithon Chapel to play the organ when there is a service. This Jones family left Lower Voil in 1946/7 and no one has lived there since. They also moved first to The Camnant, the same as the Evans family.

In the spring of 2004, Lower Voil was put on the market with seven acres of land, and there was quite a lot of interest in it. Bill, The Garn has taken Trevor over to see it, and Trevor is now 87, but he rode with Bill on the farm bike, and enjoyed his trip very much.

Bill and Joan have also taken me over — but in their Land Rover, and what a journey, but well worth it when we eventually arrived. At the end of a very long and bumpy ride across the open hill, there is quite a good track down to the house. On one side of the track there is a row of very tall, majestic-looking beech trees, then on into the fold — oh, what a sight — the most wonderful horse chestnut tree just coming out into full flower. I thought right away of the song, *Underneath the spreading chestnut tree.* To me, on that lovely sunny day, it was the perfect tree and one that I shall not forget in a hurry. I would love to go back and take a photograph. I sent to the auctioneer for details and a photograph, but no sight of a tree of any sort. I went back, just a couple of weeks later, on a wet day, and how things can change. The blossom had all blown away and my beautiful tree had shrunk to half its size, but to me it is still the perfect chestnut tree. How we see only what we want to see!

Michael and Claudi Halsey outside Lower Foel which they have now bought and have been renovating after their marriage in September 2004

I wonder what the next hundred years will be like living at Lower Voil?

Both Blaen-Voil and Blaen-cwm-Voil were quite near to Lower Voil, so they were not such isolated places as we think today. The nearest to Lower Voil was Blaen-Voil and in 1901 a Francis Pugh 37, lived there with his wife, Sarah 40, and their children, Margaret aged 11, Sarah 5, and John 2; also David Davies 62, his father-in-law.

This Pugh family were the same Pughs as George Pugh, Slate House, and Mrs. Blodwyn Brick was also one of these Pughs before she married Arthur. Most of these Pugh families were good supporters of Cwmgwyn Baptist Chapel, and Margaret, or Maggie, as we always knew her, was very generous to the little chapel. She gave several sets of fine white china tea sets with a gold rim. She also gave bone-handled tea-knives and teaspoons and half a dozen white damask tablecloths. These were all in use when I joined Cwmgwyn in 1956 and we continued to use them right up to the end of the century, when they were replaced by mugs. If there was tea at the chapel, Maggie would always be in the porch, with a bowl of hot water, washing up the dishes.

I think this Pugh family were the last to live at Blaen-Voil, and there is little left of the house today — just a clump of trees and a few stones.

Blaen-cwm-Voil was another little house quite near to the other Voils, and still in Beguildy parish. In the 1891 census, a James Davies 74, lived there with John 16, Anne 15, and George, a grandson aged 2, but I know no more about this family. Then in 1901, Richard Jones 53, his wife Martha and their sons, Alfred 26, Walter 23, Sidney 12, and Leonard 9, lived there.

Later, we hear of John Jones and his wife, Margaret Anne, living there, and they lost their first little son at three weeks old. I have heard that they had another son, but not his name. However, the father John died young at the age of 35 and was buried in Felindre old yard with their young son, William Charles, in 1913.

Later, Margaret married again, this time to Mr. Edward Davies, The Waen, but when he died in 1928, she went back home to Llanbister Road to live. She was a Tong girl, and was a distant relative of mine. When she died, she was buried in the Gravel Chapel yard next to her sister.

Maggie, John Stephens and John Davies (Gwenlas) outside Cwmgwyn Chapel

Blaen-Nanty

This is a little cottage on the side of the road going down from the crossroads to The Garn and beyond. Round about the turn of the 17th to 18th century, Blaen-Nanty was described as a 'small upland farm', although it looks very like one of our little *ty-un-nos* homesteads, with the stable joined on to the house at one end and the cowshed at the other.

I have heard that Naomi and Richard Morgan moved from Blaen-Nanty in the mid-19th century and settled at Fiddlers Green. They were

Jack, Arthur and Frank, Cissy and Stephen's three boys

a very musical family and had a great influence in the Cwmgwyn area, and especially the little chapel. Many of the families living at Blaen-Nanty seemed to have strong ties with the chapel, which perhaps is not surprising as it was the only non-conformist chapel anywhere around.

In the 1861 census, we find John and Mary Davies living there with their family, their youngest son being Stephen, who was born in 1869. This was the Stephen Davies who married Cissy Jones from Cider House, and who made Blaen-Nanty their home after they married. Their three boys — Jack, Arthur and Frank — were born there. Stephen Davies served on the Cwmgwyn Chapel Building Committee when it was formed in about 1902. While the work was going on repairing the chapel in 2000, an old Bible was found with the inscription 'Presented to the Baptist Chapel Cwmgwyn by Mrs. M. Davies, Blaen-Nanty' — this would have been Stephen's mother. The Davies family also have a book presented to Jack from Cwmgwyn Baptist Sunday School, called *Sermons in Candles* and written by C.G. Spurgeon, it is a very hard and serious book for a 12-year-old lad!

I used to have long talks with Jack about Cwmgwyn and the area around. I wish I had taken notes now, but I can remember some of the things he told me. The people living in their small cottages on the hills and moors were allowed a turnout of stock onto the open hill to graze, and apparently the hills around Cwmgwyn are blessed with a good supply of sedge-grass. The seeds of this grass are very good food for geese. However, many geese were turned out onto this hill by

Jack Penybank on one of his little Welsh ponies

day, and they needed very little extra food until it was time to start fattening them up ready for the Christmas market.

Once, Jack remembered the whole gaggle of their geese taking flight from up on the hill, whence they flew down the valley, landing at The Slopes near the top of the Hendy pitch. This was a very unusual thing for geese to do, so the three Blaen-Nanty boys were sent to run down the fields and watch where they landed, and then walk them back home. Families down the valley were allowed to walk their geese up to the Cwmgwyn hills, so it was quite normal to see them driven — but not flying!

As it came time to sell the geese for the Christmas market, many would be killed and dressed at home. The men would help with the killing and feathering, and the women with dressing and packing. A by-product from these geese were their wings which, when they were dried, would make good brushes for dusting and sweeping. In earlier times, their quills were used as pens for writing.

The geese that were not dressed at home would be driven to Newtown market and sold alive, but before they set out, they would be fitted with 'shoes'. This was done by heating tar in a flat shallow tin — not too hot — then dipping the goose's feet into the tar and holding them up until the tar had set. This was supposed to keep their feet free from blisters on the long walk to town.

Jack also told me about the little Welsh hill ponies, and there were many kept up on the hills around Cwmgwyn. These were small, strong little ponies, and were in great demand by the owners of the coalmines in South Wales. The mine-owners would come up to the Cwmgwyn area and, of course, other similar hilly areas around, trying to buy these little ponies and take them down to South Wales — a long walking trek. They would also try to tempt some of the young farm servants to come down with them and work in the mines, and many went, but we hear of some coming back a year or two later, glad to work in the open air again even if the pay was not quite so good. It was a sad day to see these little ponies taken from their native hills and their free life. It was the last time they would see the light of day, as their working days would be underground from then on. It was almost the same for the young men, but it was their choice.

I think Stephen and Cissy made full use of their turnout onto the open hill as, of course, did most families around. Geese and ponies were good moneymaking stock, and cheap to keep on the hills.

In 1924, Stephen, Cissy and family moved to Penybank, and Bill, The Garn's grandfather, Jack Lewis, moved to Blaen-Nanty. Later, his son, also Jack Lewis, moved into Blaen-Nanty with his new wife, Gertie James from The Garn. Whilst at Blaen-Nanty, their three sons were born — Emrys, Cyril and Vincent (who was always called Bill), but sadly Gertie became very ill and died when Bill was very young. Gertie's sister Nancy, who was not married, took Bill to The Garn to be brought up — and he still lives there. Cyril also went to The Garn, but Emrys went with his father to live at the Lane House with Jack's elderly mother.

A Bert Wooley and family now moved to Blaen-Nanty. They came from Yorkshire but had been living at The Nanty, in the valley just below Blaen-Nanty. During the time that this family lived at Blaen-Nanty, there was great excitement across the open hill behind Butterwell. The police had had a report of a funeral having taken place out on the hill, and they were up there looking for the grave, but all they found was a wreath. After digging down a little way, they found a small casket containing ashes, so it was put back, and all was in order. The Wooley family subsequently moved first to Kerry and then to Newtown.

Mrs. Gertie Lewis who died soon after her son Bill was born

I think our Maggie Pugh then moved to Blaen-Nanty, but her move was followed not long after by the very bad snowstorm of 1963 and Maggie found it difficult to cope on her own, so Cyril brought her to The Garn to be looked after by Nancy and Joan.

Tim and Alice Lewis with their daughter Maisie were next to live here, but soon moved on to Maesyrhelem farm. They used to attend Cwmgwyn Chapel while at Blaen-Nanty, and Maisie came back in 2004 to the Anniversary.

Mervyn Davies and his wife Bronwen were the next couple to live at Blaen-Nanty. Mervyn was a grandson for Cissy and Stephen Davies, and Mervyn's father, Arthur, who had lived here himself many years ago, still owned the property. The young couple first lived in a caravan near to the house, presumably while a few alterations and repairs were carried out in the house. They then moved into the house for a period, but later went to live in the Bucknell area.

Now Miss Hamer, a real character and used to ride a motorbike, moved here from The Trefoil. She had some comical stories to tell about taking her road test on her bike. On one test, the examiner stopped her and asked her to take the last part of the triangular section of the test course, but to do it in reverse. 'Don't be silly, man, there is no reverse gear on a motorbike,' said Miss Hamer. Another time, taking the test in the winter, when the weather was looking very like for snow, the examiner asked her what would she do if there was snow on the road? 'Stay at home,' said Miss Hamer. I think both answers were very sensible, but I don't think she ever passed her motorbike test.

Miss Hamer moved from Blaen-Nanty to The Sign, Llanbadarn and later to a little house in the village, and Blaen-Nanty was left empty for a few years. Then Owen Roberts, his wife Freda, and their children, Anne and Brian, moved in. Christopher, their youngest son, was born at Blaen-Nanty.

Freda and Owen Roberts with their three children: Bryan, Ann and Christopher

Owen had a contracting business and used to go around farms spreading slag, lime and other fertilizers. He was spreading slag at The Waen once for Doug, and at the end of the day he came to the house to enquire if we needed any more work doing while he had all the machinery there. He was still wearing his goggles and mask, and some of our boys ran to the door to see who was there. Owen then took off his goggles and mask to talk, but the boys ran back in to me, saying there was a man from the moon at the door. Poor Owen, he did look a strange man, with a black face and white around his eyes and mouth, but he tried to rub some of the slag off his face to show the boys he was really a white man. After that, he was always called 'the Moon Man'.

In 1982 Owen bought the Blacksmith's Shop in Felindre. They were the last people to live in Blaen-Nanty house. Arthur later sold the property to Wynford Lewis, Springfield, and he uses the house as a storage shed, whilst farming the land.

Owen is usually seen walking down the road on a Sunday afternoon to the Baptist chapel in Felindre, and the two boys attend the Methodist chapel in Llanbister. However, they come back to Cwmgwyn on special services such as the Anniversary, Songs of Praise and Harvest — even Anne, her husband and their two children — and it's good to see them all.

Towards the end of 2004 Blaen-Nanty has been named as a 'listed building', although it seems a bit late as it is now in a rather sorry state. However, some of the 'powers that be' have written to the present owner with this surprising information.

Springfield

This is a modern house built in 1968 very near to the site where Penfynon had been. Cyril and Bill, The Garn, had it built for their father, Jack Lewis, who had started his married life at Blaen-Nanty in the mid-1920s but had lost his wife whilst living there. When the new house at Springfield was nearly finished, sadly Jack died, so Cyril and Auntie Nancy, The Garn, moved in. A few years later, Auntie fell and broke her leg, so she went back to The Garn to be looked after by Joan and Bill. Cyril had married a girl from St. Harmon, but I don't think she ever lived at Springfield. She stayed at her home and worked on the family farm. They had a son, Wynford, who spent his early years with his mother, and then when he left school at the age of 16, he came to Springfield to help his dad on the farm.

In 1984 Cyril bought the ground belonging to Butterwell, which was now owned by Mrs. Koreen Davies, Bwlch-y-llyn. Then, in 1985, he bought Blaen-Nanty from Arthur Davies, a son for the Davies family, Penybank, so Springfield is now a good-sized farm, especially with the turn-outs onto the open hill from these two properties.

Wynford married Robin, a Cardiff girl who used to come up to Llanbadarn to visit her auntie, who had herself married Alan Morris. They have two children — Bethan, who now has a little girl, Kathryn, and who live in Knighton; and Matthew, who is still in the Secondary Modern School in Llandrindod Wells. Robin has, for many years, transported the children from around this area — Gwenlas, The Ddol, Dolfryn and their own — to Llanbadarn to meet the school bus, which then takes the younger children to Llanbister School and the older ones to Llandrindod. In days gone by there was a school at Llaithddu where the children could stay until they were sixteen and then go straight out to work. There was also Glan Ithon School just below Llanbadarn, as well as Primary Schools at Llanddewi and Llanbister, but now only Llanbister School remains open, from where children leave at around 11 years old and go to the Secondary Modern in Llandrindod Wells.

Robin and their children are involved in the local Young Farmers' movement, and belong to the Llanbadarn club, but just lately, because of smaller numbers in each club, they join with Teme Valley club and enter competitions together.

Springfield, built in 1968. Robin is pictured with granddaughter Kathryn and Wynford, Bethan and Matthew

The Young Farmers' Club is a country organization and is of great benefit to the country children, some of whom would otherwise have a quiet, and maybe, sheltered life. It's a very good meeting place for the youth, and taking part in the competitions must give them confidence and, of course, the chance to learn new skills which can be invaluable for life. Also, as with the walk to churches and chapels years ago, many find their partners for life in the Y.F.C. Today, some of our clubs are getting smaller because some areas just have not got the population they had some twenty or thirty years ago, but we hope that the Y.F.C. movement will continue and that the country people will support it.

The Garn

The Garn house, as we know it today, was built around 1850 for the James family, Cwmllechwyd, and descendants of that family are still living there today. The old Garn house was just out across the meadow, but is now only a few stones and a crab apple tree. Although The Garn is in Llanbadarn Fynydd parish, it has from early days had strong connections with Cwmgwyn Baptist Chapel. Around the turn of the century, James James — who was never married — is mentioned as being on the building committee of the chapel. This committee was formed to try to buy the little Wesleyan chapel, which was closing down, and change it into a Baptist chapel. In those days, it was half its present size so they also planned to extend it. They were successful and we find that James James, The Garn, was a Sunday School teacher for several years.

The cover and inside pages of the memory card given to all who attended James James's funeral. The last one I have seen was at Ella Stephens's funeral in 1965

"In Loving Memory"

"We have to mourn the loss of one,
We did our best to save;
Beloved on earth, regretted, gone.
Remembered in the grave."

"Thou shalt come to thy grave in a full age, like as a shock of corn cometh in in his season." Job 5. 26.

In Loving Memory
of
JAMES JAMES,
of The Garn, Llanbadarn,
Who passed peacefully away on October 9th, 1934,
Aged 80 Years.

Interred at Llananno Churchyard.

James James' sister, Martha, married a Pryce from The Ddol, Llanbadarn, and they lived at The Garn. Their children were Jinnie, Mary Anne (who was always known as Nancy), Gladys, Gertie and Tommy. Later, Jinnie, Gladys and Gertie got married and moved away. Gertie married John Lewis, the Hendre, and they moved to Blaen-Nanty. While there, their three sons were born — Emrys, Cyril and Vincent (or Bill, as he was always called). Sadly, while Bill was still young, Gertie died, and Cyril and Bill went to The Garn to be brought up by Nancy and Tommy, and Emrys went with his father to live at the Lane House with John's mother.

Bill went to the Llaithddu school, riding pony-back up to Crochen, after which he cut across the field to the school. If the river was in flood, he would walk across the footbridge and let the pony swim across. Teddy Botwood from the Nanty was his companion, and I expect they would meet up with others on the way. People often used to travel together in those days, whereas today we jump in a car and talk to no one.

Bill remembers going to Cwmgwyn when he was a lad, especially on Anniversary days. The chapel would be full and its grounds crowded with young girls and boys. On fine days, he remembers, even the lane to the main road would be full of young lads. What fun they would have, throwing small stones onto the roof to roll down with a big noise. Once, they picked green gooseberries and threw them through the door, and even caught a goose and put that in. Harmless pranks, and the goose could give back better than it got!

Sometimes, the boys would wire up the gates on the smaller roads, and there were many of those, so that when the young ladies came along they would have to climb over. This seemed to give the boys great enjoyment as they followed behind, and even the girls seemed happy with it all.

Ice up near The Garn in 1996. If you shook the fence, the ice would fall off just like glass falling out of a pane in a window

People, especially the young folk, would walk for miles to an Anniversary. They would come to Cwmgwyn from Bwlchsarnau, Llaithddu, Llanbadarn, Maesyrhelem, Mochdre, Dolfor, Kerry — and all places between. Then when another chapel held their Anniversary, the crowd would walk there. This was part of our 'growing up' time and we got to know many other young folk living around. Later, some of us found our partner for life on these walks.

There was no telly or cinema in those days — only the wireless, and we were not allowed to listen to that for long. It was the 'News' and the 'Meteorological forecast'. This always amazed me, as my father, who had a bad stammer, could get through both words without any hesitation. He would send us into the house from the hayfield to turn the wireless on at 11.00 a.m., then run back to the field to tell him if it was going to rain. Sometimes we would be allowed to listen to 'Monday Night at Eight' and later 'The Archers'. As we grew older, we didn't want to use it for long, as we had to carry the heavy old accumulators to a garage to have them charged up, and if you spilt anything on your clothes it would burn a hole.

Bill Lewis remembers cutting and collecting gorse and heather to heat up the bread oven, as these gave a quick, hot heat. Then they would cut turf and stack it up to dry, later loading it onto a cart and taking it home to store in a dry barn for winter fuel. He also remembers cutting the heather as long as the stalk would allow, taking it home and weaving it up through the netting sides of the wain-house, starting at the bottom. The bushy flowers would be left, then the next stalk would start just above the flowers, until the whole wall was covered and would be wind- and rain-proof. How clever and ingenious they were in those days to make the best use of materials growing around them.

In 1957 Bill married a Mochdre girl, Joan Morgan, and they lived at The Garn with Nancy and Tommy. Bill and Joan have two children, Erfyl and Thelma. Erfyl married Tracy Thomas from Dolfor and they have built a new house on Garn ground just below Cwm-mawr. They both work on the farm, and have two children, Hannah and Bryn. Thelma married Andrew Powell and lives near Newtown. They have two sons, Lee and Daniel — both good footballers.

Joan and Bill have always been very loyal supporters of

Thelma, an American student, Erfyl, Joan and Bill

Cwmgwyn Chapel, along with many other chapels in the area. Joan is a good singer and started singing duets with my husband, Doug Thomas, The Waen. They both had good, true voices and blended well together. They first sang at Llanbadarn to entertain guests at the Farmers' Union dinner, then started singing at Cwmgwyn and other places around. A few years later they were two of the founder members of the Dolithon Choir. Joan was our treasurer, and still is, thirty years later. We must have sung in hundreds of churches, chapels, village halls and hospitals. One year we had fifty-six concerts with the full choir at every one. The choir has helped to raise hundreds, if not thousands of pounds for charity, and also to help keep a little chapel open for a few more years.

Nancy lived at The Garn with Bill and Joan up to her death in 1983 at the age of 87. She was a dear lady, with a kind word for everyone. Auntie Nancy, as on most farms, kept a lot of poultry, especially geese. I can remember the yard at The Garn nearly full of geese, and what a noise if a stranger came near! As Christmas drew close, it would be a very busy time. The men would help with the killing and feathering, and the women with dressing and packing ready for market. Neighbours and friends would come to help and it would be turned into a social gathering with plenty of food and drink, continuing well into the night with plenty of laughter and talking.

Bill and Joan have, I think, been very happy living at The Garn — Bill, for all of his life. They enjoy the values of yesteryear, and also modern day living in the country. There is always a warm welcome for all at The Garn, and I feel that the area up the top of the valley would be a poorer place without them.

The lost homes on the hills above Cwmgwyn

There were several other little places on the hills between Blaen-Nanty and Penybank, and I am just going to mention them so that you will see that a hundred or more years ago there were many people living up on the hills around Cwmgwyn. I think it was a poor area in terms of money, but I think it was a happy place and everyone knew their neighbours for miles around and were willing to lend a helping hand — even to giving food and clothes to those in need.

Penfynon was a little house very near to where the new house Springfield has been built, but there is no trace of it today. Billy Davies and family lived there around the turn of the century. He was the gentleman who was annoyed at the donkeys that were kept at The Waen while the new house was being built. The bricks for the house were made in a field under Fiddlers Green and brought up to The Waen by donkey-cart, so I suppose some of these donkeys would have been hired or borrowed to do the job, so would be in new surroundings and with new mates, and would be rather noisy for a few weeks, thus keeping Billy awake. I have also heard about his young daughter who was still at school, carrying her little brother all the way to The Green, Llanbadarn, where I think their grandparents lived. This would be a very long distance over rough hills, but in those days we were all used to walking miles and carrying heavy loads.

I think Morley Jones, Maesgwyn's family lived here after Billy Davies. Bill, The Garn, remembers taking Morley out onto the hill to collect heather to put on his mother's grave. The Wooley family also lived here for a short while before moving to Blaen-Nanty.

Simons was another little house in the dingle under The Garn, and a Woosnam lived here, then a Tom Pryce — related to Tom Pryce, Cwm-mawr. He once came to The Garn to beg for a swede to cook with their Christmas dinner.

Further along in the valley was The Nanty. Teddy Botwood lived here and went to Llaithddu School with Bill, The Garn. He later moved to Gystogen, which is in a very wild area above Ddully Bank in the Llaithddu. Teddy once came to Denmark on one of our choir trips, when we saw a different side to Ted — he was so interested in their methods of farming, and asked such sensible questions that we were all amazed, and the Danes thought he was great. When it came time to board the ship to come home we were stopped by Customs and

Billy Davies (The Green), son for James and Elizabeth (Lluest)

Teddy Botwood, Bill Stephens and Doug Thomas having Danish farming explained to them

Excise. Our bus was searched to the extent that the interior panels were taken off — but they found nothing. Then it was our turn to walk through Customs, and how Ted and his friend, Bill Stephens, got through, I shall never know. Their socks, shoes and all other clothing had packets of 'bacco bulging out everywhere, but they got through. It was a nerve-racking couple of hours, but caused a great deal of laughter and excitement after. The only item we had to pay duty on was one bottle of whisky, which poor Cynthia Davies, one of our choir members, had above the limit.

Then there was Cwm-Nanty where a Hughes family lived. They were related to John Hughes, the School House, Llaithddu, and nearer Blaen-Nanty was The Guifron where, years ago, three grown-up brothers died of a fever. This used to happen in those days as there would be no inoculations or antibiotics, and sometimes whole families would be wiped out, especially the children. Diphtheria and scarlet fever were two very serious illnesses in children, and sometimes the school would close down for weeks. Certain types of influenza were killers for grown-ups, too.

And so the hilly area up on the top where the main Llandrindod to Newtown road ran was quite a busy place, but today all trace of these houses has disappeared.

The base of Cilvaesty Hill

The Prysg
This is a little cottage up the lane above the Hendy, and most probably when it was built would have been a little ty-un-nos. The builders who renovated and modernised it in 2001 uncovered a beam above the fireplace dated 1706, which also had the carved initials M.C. and C.P., possibly those of the carpenter and the builder. I have heard that a beam with the same carved initials and date was found in Friesland, so many of these little *ty-un-nos* homesteads could have been built around that time.

The first mention in the census forms of anyone living at the Prysg was in 1844, when a Richard Morgan lived there, but the owner of the property was Sir Francis Howe Seymour Knowles, 5th Baronet of Knowles. It just amazes me that such a titled man should have even come to Radnorshire, let alone to own a little place like the Prysg, but I cannot find out any more about him. Anyway, he still owned it in 1886. Was it, I wonder, that rich men needed to get away to gain some peace and quiet as, of course, today some people with plenty of money are coming out of the big towns and buying small properties and enjoying the peace.

In 1850 Anne Pryce lived there with her four children. They were classed as 'paupers' in the census form, so possibly she had lost her husband through ill health or an accident, and could claim help from the parish to bring up her chil-

The Prysg before renovations started, with (below) the house and family today

dren. Later, a John Evans, his wife Mary and their six children lived there. Also, Margaret Stephens, Cwmgwyn Hall heard from a family living in America who said that they used to live at the Prysg. Then in the 1891 census, Anne Benbow and her two little children lived there. Anne was the widow of a blacksmith, which in those days was a dangerous job, for whilst horses and ponies can be good friends, they also have a very powerful kick, and was the cause of many an accident.

The first family that anyone around today remembers living there was Charlie Morgan, his wife Sarah and their children — Alice, William, Margaret, Elsie, Jane, Fanny and Rene. Charlie was the gentleman who was always worried about that black cloud hanging over the top of Cilvaesty Hill. He was a member of Cwmgwyn Chapel, as were most of his family.

I think this family was the last to live at the Prysg. The property was then sold to their neighbour, the Stephens family, who then used the house as winter shelter for the cattle, and hay and straw were stored in the bedrooms.

In 2001 Alwena Stephens, Cwmgwyn Hall, and Charles Campbell were married in Felindre Baptist Chapel, and they decided to make the Prysg their home. They had it all modernised and renovated, but still kept it near to its original size, although the stable on one side and a shed on the other side have been added into the house. The beam which the builders found now straddles their new Aga stove. And so one little *ty-un-nos* home has been saved and lives to tell the tale. Llanmadog, in Beguildy, is another one, which has changed back from cattle to people living there.

In November 2003, we heard great news — Alwena and Charlie had a little daughter, Ella Grace. So new life is coming once again to the Cwmgwyn area and giving hope for the future, just as Alwena, John and Ruth did only a few years ago, when they were born. How time flies — a generation seems no time, as we grow older.

Panty-Beudy

This is quite a large farmhouse at the base of Cilvaesty Hill. The road to it these days is across the lane to the Hendy, then up that very steep hill, through the gate, then across on the right hand side along a rough road. The Prysg, Tynllwyn and Llethrau Cottage are all quite near, so it is not as isolated as we might think, but whilst they are all beautiful places to live in the summer, a hard winter, with ice and snow,

The Martin family arrive at Panty-Beudy (top) and start work on the house. How brave they were!

sometimes makes that steep bank difficult, if not impossible. I have heard that it was never quite finished when it was first built, and the front door could not be used — it stood about four feet up the wall, with no steps up to it.

In the 1891 census, a William Pryce 35, lived there with his wife Jane 25, and three children, Mary Lloyd 3, Jane Lloyd 2, and Elizabeth Pryce 1, so Jane must have lost or left her husband and wasted no time in finding a new husband and having his child. Life for a woman with children was very hard in those days, especially if she had no means of an income, or could not live at home with her parents. They were recorded as paupers, and would be partly kept by the Parish.

In the 1901 census, a James Lewis 44, farmer, his wife Mary, also 44, and their children, Mary 19, George 17, Martin 16, Jessie 10, and Maybelle 9, lived there. This family used to come to Cwmgwyn Chapel. James died in 1905 and is buried in Felindre Baptist — the old yard. He was only 49 years old and his wife died in 1920 aged 63, and is buried with him. I have heard that one of the men in this family was tragically drowned in a stream up by the house, but I do not know which one or why. The two sons died in 1950 — George in the April aged 66 and Martin, who had married a Gertrude Margaret from Pound Gate, died in the December aged 65.

I think that Tom Hamer now bought the farm, and then sold the house to an airline pilot from London. By this time the house needed a lot of work and money spending on it to make it fit for living in, and it was sold on to Robin Martin and family. Robin was a builder, so he set about rebuilding and repairing, the family living in a caravan while the work was going on. In the summer, instead of carrying water up to the van, they would all go down to the river to get themselves, and their clothes, washed.

The whole of the front wall had to be rebuilt, when the opportunity was taken to turn the front door into a window, and a new door was made in the side wall, with steps up to it. Robin also re-roofed the house and had the water put in and fires going, and then they moved into the house.

Wash-day in the river (left) and finished at last (right)

Panty-Beudy is now a fine house

The children came to Beguildy School while I was there — Rebecca, Emma and Robin, but I think Victoria must have gone to John Beddoes, Presteigne. Roz, the mother, used to come to school to help me with the Infant Class, and one year she made new costumes for the Christmas Nativity play, which we used for many years, and I think some may be still in use.

Robin and some of his building friends once made a playhouse for the children. We painted it cream with a red door and called it 'Robin's Nest'. It was in use for many years at school, and then it could be seen on David Barrett's lawn, but I think it has, at last, disintegrated. Anyway, many thanks to Roz and Robin for their help.

The Martin family left Panty-Beudy in the mid-1980s and have turned a large old house in Knighton into a Nursing Home for old folks, which is still well used today.

Geoff and Carolyn Duthie, who had kept the Wharf Inn in Felindre for about ten years, bought Panty-Beudy and moved up there with their three children — Helen, Bill and Joe. They have been busy making some internal alterations to suit their family, and have also built a veranda right across the front of the house, with a carport underneath. This seems a very good idea, as they have pots of plants and flowers just outside their sitting room windows, and the cars underneath are dry and out of the snow and frost in the winter.

Their children are now all married and left home. Helen married a local boy, Stephen Reynolds, Black House, and they have four children — Charlie, Kate, Bill and Alfie — and they live in the village. Bill married Alison Slater, a Newtown girl, and they have three boys — Bill, Robert and Thomas — and Joe has married Michelle, a Liverpool girl, and they have two children, Sam and Lauren.

Geoff and Carolyn still live at Panty-Beudy and still go out to work, Carolyn in Laura Ashley in Newtown and Geoff is a salesman. They are both very much into gardening and have a wonderful display of flowers on the veranda and others growing around — also two greenhouses to give the plants a good start. It is so quiet and peaceful up there, with only the birds and bees to listen to. Only for that steep bank, it is a wonderful place to live.

Tynllwyn

This is another little house up on the hill above the Hendy, but it is on the side of a good road, so has had people living in it for most of the time.

The first people we hear of living there in the 1891 census were Thomas Edward 68, his wife Mary 61, and Thomas their son 26. By 1901 these people have moved away and John Williams 40, a son from Yrchyn, his wife Jane 37, Alfred Owen and Mary Owen, stepchildren and Sarah Williams, their daughter aged eight months, lived there. This couple subsequently had more children, including a daughter called Lucy, who married a Victor Pugh. This young couple then moved into Tynllwyn, and John and Jane Williams and their family moved down to the Vron Mill.

Victor and Lucy had three sons — Ernie and Maurice, who moved to Clee Hill to work and Clifford, who when he grew up, used to go out shearing with his father,

Above: Victor and Lucy Pugh who lived at Tynllwyn, then moved down to Vron Mill when their son, Clifford, got married.
Left: Victor Pugh. One year he won the Crankshaw Cup at the sheepdog trails at Llanbadarn, which he retained for a year

Cliford and Olwen were married in 1950 and they moved down to Dutlas to the Old Carpenter's Shop

Victor. They did all the shearing for the Lloyds, The Llethrau, for several years running but were not allowed to start until after 12th July, which Clifford told me was called Dog Day. This was because if they accidentally cut a sheep before that date, the wound would not heal, but would go septic and the sheep possibly die. The Lloyds also rented the ground in Newtown at the golf-links. These sheep were a better breed of sheep and could be shorn much earlier. Clifford and his dad also helped to shear Bright's, Upper House, and other places around if they needed help. Victor won the Crankshaw Cup one year at the Sheep Dog trials at Llanbadarn.

Clifford on the binder with a land girl on the tractor — possibly Elsie?

Clifford married Olwen Williams from Newcwm and in 1950 they moved down to the carpenter's shop in Dutlas. They are still living there and have just celebrated their Golden Wedding. They have one son, Malcolm, who married Helen and they live in Beguildy with their two daughters, Monique and Lisa.

The next family we hear of living at Tynllwyn are Horace Frances and his wife Muriel and Harold Frances, a son for Horace and stepson for Muriel. This family moved down from Yorkshire. Harold was a very helpful lad, especially at Sports and other functions. He now lives in Clun. Horace died in 1957, aged 49, and is buried in Crug-y-Byddar Church yard.

Later, Muriel married Albert Reynolds, a son for Irene and Thomas Reynolds, Cwmbugail, and they had a son, Nigel. They continued to live at Tynllwyn for a few years, then moved to Banbury in 1965.

Tom Hamer then bought Tynllwyn, and lived and farmed there for several years. Tom became very friendly with London folk who had bought Llethrau Cottage and I think had many trips up to London and elsewhere with them. Then Tom retired and moved to Newtown and his nephew Stephen George from Penarron, Kerry, farms the land. The house is let to David and Jayne Penlington. David works on the farm with Stephen and Jayne now is a helper in a Nursing Home in Rhayader. After living at Tynllwyn for four years, they have now moved to Kerry, but David still works for Stephen on the farm. Tynllwyn is now let to a couple from Montgomery who are friends of Mary and Iain Plummer in the village.

Llethrau Cottage

This is another little cottage out on the hill beyond Tynllwyn and the Prysg, which is being used as a holiday cottage, although it has no road, no electric, and no phone, as Doug and I found out when we took over the Post Office in 1979. We would often have to take telegrams up there and it was always a 'welly' job, as it was mud and fields for the end of the journey.

In the 1891 census the house was occupied by a carpenter by the name of John Lewis 40, his wife Sarah 39, Lavinia 3, and 1-year-old Pryce, along with Margaret Jenkins 63, John's mother-in-law. By 1901 this family had moved down to the Gravel and Charles Morgan 32, general workman, his wife Sarah 24, Alice 5, William 2, and Margaret, four months old, had taken over. In the 1891 census this Charlie Morgan was working for John Lloyd at The Llethrau. He was also a member at Cwmgwyn and was always worried about that black cloud hanging over Cilvaesty Hill. Later Charlie and family moved to the Prysg.

Mr. and Mrs. Evans, related to Mrs. Stephens, The Hendy, lived at Llethrau Cottage for a while, then a Richard Turner and his wife, Janet, bought it in 1972. This couple spent a lot of time and money repairing and improving it, but they never lived there and sold it in about 1976 to Mr. and Mrs. Weiss as a holiday cottage.

At that time this couple had two children, and they also fostered two coloured children — Monica and Jo. They were from London and would come out on the train to Newtown, and then take a taxi up to the cottage. They came out often in the beginning when the children were young, and about mid-week they would all walk down to the shop and buy bags of shopping which they would then carry up those steep hills back to the house. This family still comes out, especially the children with their friends, and it is good to see some of these old dwellings being used and enjoyed.

Tom Hamer became very friendly with the Weiss family, and I hear that he has been seen strolling down the streets of London in days gone by! They were very good friends and Mr. and Mrs. Weiss would often come to Newtown, meet up with Tom and take him out for a meal.

In 2004 Mr. Weiss died, as did Tom Hamer. Several of the Weiss family and friends came out to Felindre to Tom's funeral. I think they have lost a good friend.

The Llethrau

In the 1891 census we find John Lloyd 27, a farmer, living at The Llethrau, with his brother Thomas 26, nephew Evan 32, sister Anne 12, and Mary 55, his stepmother and housekeeper. The household also included three servants — Charlie Morgan 23, Thomas Williams 18, and Mary Jones 18 — and staying there was Sarah Jones 68, a visitor.

In the 1901 census, John Lloyd 37, is still there with his wife Mary 28. (I wonder, was that the domestic servant, Mary Jones, aged 18 in 1891?) There were also two sons, John 8, and Thomas 1. Evan was still there as was Thomas Owens 33, a servant; Pryce Jandrell 18, a servant from Mochdre; George Hughes 34, a servant from Llanbister; and Sarah Lewis 24, a servant from Llananno.

It seems The Llethrau was a very busy place, and there were a lot of people for a small house. But I've been told that the farm then consisted of about two hundred acres, so all those men would be needed. Perhaps some would sleep out in the barns, as this was often the sleeping quarters for servant boys in those days.

In 1932 the Lloyds were still there. I have been talking to Mr. Walter Bufton, who in 1932, when only a lumper, was hired from Knighton May Fair by Cecil Lloyd, The Llethrau. His pay was £14 for the year! Walter only worked there for one year, but he remembers several things about The Llethrau, although he is now 85 years old. John Lloyd and his son, Cecil, were still farming the land and kept many cattle, and Walter remembers some of the bullocks had horns so long that they had to turn their heads sideways in order to get through the doors of the shed in winter-time. He also remembers Cecil telling him that if ever he got lost out on the hills around Cwmgwyn while riding his pony, to put the reins on the pony's neck and he'd get home safely. Walter was very glad of that advice once when he was lost in fog up around Butterwell. He just let go of the reins and put them on the pony's neck, to be taken back to the gate by Cilvaesty tump, as near to The Llethrau as he could go.

Maggie Pugh was housekeeper at that time, and he says it was always a dish of stodgy steam pudding first before the meat and potatoes. This was to fill you up!

Walter was a great friend of Gilbert Pugh, Slate House, and used to go to Cwmgwyn Chapel with him often on a Sunday. He even recited there on the Anniversary 'Oh, the best book to read is the Bible' (one of the Sankey hymns).

Another little memory, which even now makes him laugh, was when they were going out from dinner Cecil would often run after them and shout 'Do as much as you can today, boys, because we are going to be very busy tomorrow.' However, it seems that the Lloyds' 'tomorrow' didn't start very early, then come eight or nine at night and they were full of work.

Walter remembers Pryce Lewis, a carpenter, at the Gravel, as well as Fred Davies, the postman from Dolfrynog, who had some hurdles wired up as gates. Cecil always called these 'havers'.

Many folk up around the Bettws way remember Walter as their school bus-driver for many years. Gwyneth, the Moat's father also worked at The Llethrau during the 1930s.

When war broke out in 1939, the Ministry of Defence commandeered The Llethrau as a military base, and old Mr. Lloyd and Cecil moved to Persandy, and farmed there. John Mills, his wife Myfanwy, and two of their children, Reuben and Mary, moved to The Llethrau from Little House, and Glenys stayed with the two older relations, Reuben and Jane Morgan, at the Little House.

During and after the war, all farms had, by law, to plough up acres of land and grow crops to help feed the nation, as we could not import food during the war. The farms in these hilly areas up around The Llethrau, and indeed all farms on high ground, were ordered to grow potatoes, as this is a crop comparatively suitable for hilly ground.

John Mills was put in charge of prisoners of war, firstly the Italians, then later the Germans. One or sometimes two lorry loads of these P.O.W.s would be brought up to The Llethrau in the morning from the camp in Presteigne and taken back there at night. John had to get them all working and often the work was planting or picking potatoes. This was a tedious and back-breaking job, as I well remember, but it needed no skills, so these prisoners could get straight in working. Sometimes a lorry load of Land Army girls would also be brought up there. Mrs. Elsie George, who was a Lancashire lass, remembers going to The Llethrau and picking potatoes with these P.O.W.s. When it came time for dinner, these lads would have a fire with a large pot of potatoes boiling ready for their dinners, and they would be always asking the girls to try to bring some salt up with them the following day. So it seems that I am not the only one who likes salt boiled in with my vegetables. The young mums of today use but very little, if any, salt in their cooking. It is thought to be not good for our health.

Salt is mentioned several times in the Bible, and also the Romans used to come up from the east coast into Wales to mine lead ore and take it back to make large dishes. Then they would boil sea water in these dishes, and when all of the water had evaporated, they were left with salt. Soon after we had moved to Felindre a Professor at Cambridge University called at the shop and asked, 'Where is the Teme Bridge?' I took him down the road to the bridge, which is not actually the Teme Bridge! He said that the Romans used to come up to that bridge in a canoe – damming the Teme in three places between Leintwardine and Felindre. They would climb up a hill to the lead mine, (which is up near Marpoles, the Llanarch), and mine the lead to take back to the East coast to get their salt. At that time I told people about this, but I think most thought I was going round the bend, but a couple of years ago Richard Brock's father sent me a cutting from a guide book which read as follows:

> The Iron Age and Roman salt collectors found it easy to evaporate salt from the brine using small wood fired ovens and shallow dishes. The Romans used dishes made from lead sheets roughly five feet by three feet. The lead came from mines in the Plynlimon area of Wales and was shipped down the River Severn. A large lead mine also existed at Felindre on the upper reaches of the Teme.

It looks from this that I wasn't going round the bend after all, so thanks, Mr. Brock, Senior, for restoring faith in myself.

Elsie also remembers threshing up at The Llethrau, and of course, at many other farms. Sid George, The Moat, would be on the threshing box, and the girls would be his helpers, some bringing the sheaves of corn from the ricks for Sid to put through the box, while another group would be bagging up the grain and tying up the straw. Most jobs on the farms in those days were done by hand. Later, Elsie and Sid were married in Felindre Baptist Chapel with Mary Morris organising their reception in the schoolroom at the back of the chapel, and they have lived in Beguildy ever since. Elsie's mother came to live in Beguildy, near to Elsie, and lived to be 101 years old. She used to make some beautiful crochet items.

In 1945, John and Myfanwy Mills had their second son, Douglas, and soon after that, they moved to Medwaledd.

Elsie and Sid George on their wedding day

Cecil Lloyd then moved back to The Llethrau. His father, John, died in 1945, aged 81. His mother, Mary, had died in 1920 at the age of 48, and also a brother, Marsh, died in 1923, aged 30. This young death was the result of a septic wound. Cecil died in 1963 at the age of 63 and they are all buried in Crug-y-Byddar Church yard.

The Llethrau was now sold to Fountains Farmers, who also bought Medwaledd. They then sold The Llethrau house and farmed the land. A young couple, Sue and Stephen Yorke, bought the house and spent a lot of time and money repairing and renovating it but it was well done and in keeping with its age. In 1978 they sold it to Mrs. Elizabeth Holmes, who had sold her farm in Ireland and she moved into The Llethrau and is still living there today.

In the mid '80s the folk from Cwmgwyn Chapel decided to raise money for Cancer Research, as a friend of the chapel was suffering from the illness. We had a short service in the chapel, then walked up to The Llethrau, as they used to do many years before. When we got our

Elsie and Sid George on their tractor with the threshing box behind

Raising money for Cancer Research. After a short service in the chapel and a long walk up to Llethrau, we had a sing-song and tea provided by Mrs. Elizabeth Holmes. Mrs. Sheila Morgan, a cancer sufferer, received our donations

breath back, we had a good old Sankey sing-song in the garden. Mrs. Holmes and her family then brought round tea for all of us. It was a lovely day.

Some time later in harvest time, there was a fire at The Llethrau, the main damage being to the kitchen and the roof. The Hendre boys were harvesting in the field above the house and, noticing smoke coming from the house, ran down to help. Elizabeth managed to get nearly all her furniture out with help from neighbours and the boys.

Elizabeth has done an amazing job on the garden. She improved the soil by collecting and using the soil from mole hills, her young grandchildren, Phoebe and Thomas, helping in the task. The barn has been turned into a living area for family and friends when they visit.

In 2000 Mrs. Glithyn Gough organised an 'Open Garden Sunday' with the proceeds going to the Royal Welsh Show. This was a great success as The Llethrau, although quite a distance off the beaten track, proved to be a very popular place to visit. In 2004 Elizabeth had a hip replacement operation and stayed with her daughter in Richmond for the winter. However, she is now back at The Llethrau and organising the garden again. She really is a remarkable lady.

Medwaledd

In the 1891 census, farmer James Pugh 39, his wife Eliza 36, David 14, Mary 12, James 11, John 10, Sarah 8, Pryce 6, Frances 4, Arthur 2, and Gwendoline 1, all lived here. James, or Jimmy as he was called, came up from South Wales and had his 'own account', having saved a small amount of money presumably from working in the coalmines for a while. He married a Llanbadarn girl, Eliza.

In the 1901 census they were all there still and all ten years older. There were also two more daughters, Rozanne 9, and Miriam 7. What a family! Jimmy used to call them 'his little rabbits'. They farmed at Medwaledd for many years.

Before Cwmgwyn Chapel was built, I have been told that there was a little chapel at Medwaledd, just about

James and Eliza Pugh. They lived at Medwaledd and had 11 children, which Jimmy called 'his little rabbits'

where Tom Harris has built his cattle sheds. Jimmy and his family were loyal members of Cwmgwyn, and was a member of the Building Committee. When the extension was built in 1908, he was made a trustee. Eliza died at Medwaledd in 1924 aged 69, and Jimmy then moved to Cwmheyope where he died in 1930, also aged 69. Both are buried in Felindre 'new yard'.

It seems that John Lloyd and his son, Cecil, then acquired Medwaledd and rented it out to a relation of theirs, Henry Jones of Sarn. Mary Pugh, Gilbert Pugh's sister from Slate House, went to keep house for him. Later Henry and Mary were married and they lived at Medwaledd for several years. While there, Daisy and Dorothy were born, and when Dorothy grew up she married Richard Gough and they now live at New House, Newcastle. The girls and their mother were very good supporters of Cwmgwyn Chapel, and Dorothy has been very helpful with the history of Slate House, where her grandparents used to live. Henry, Mary and family moved out of Medwaledd in 1938.

In the early part of the Second World War, Mr. and Mrs. Richards, Hope's Castle, moved to Medwaledd with their youngest daughter, Rowena, while their son, John, stayed on at Hope's Castle to farm, and is still there today.

While at Medwaledd, Mr. and Mrs. Richards worked for the Ministry of Defence and were asked to have a prisoner of war to help farm the land, and live in the house with them. At first such P.O.W.s were Italian, then later German. I can remember that at our home, the first P.O.W. was an Italian named Joe. He was a happy-go-lucky chap, with not much idea of farm work — nor, indeed, of any other manual work, but as children we used to have a lot of fun with Joe, and after the war he came back to Wales to see us. Next we had a German lad, who was a good worker but very quiet and sullen. I think he was quite a young lad and spoke no

Medwaledd

Left to right: Myfanwy Davies, Neville Huffer, E. Huffer, Thomas Huffer, Eric Huffer, Margaret Mills, John Mills, Myfanwy Mills and Barbara Jones, with Paul Evans as the Page Boy

English, so he must have been terrified, and as children, we were warned not to have much to do with him. I think we were all a bit afraid of him.

As the war came to an end, Mr. and Mrs. Richards retired and moved into the Old Post Office in Felindre, next door to the manse. These two houses have now been made into one and Barbara and George Barrett live in it.

The next family to move into Medwaledd were Jack and Myfanwy Mills and their youngest children, Reuben, Mary and baby Doug who was born in 1945 at The Llethrau. This couple had been living at Little House with Reuben Morgan and his sister, Jane, who were children of Naomi and Richard Morgan, Fiddlers Green, and both Jack and Myfanwy were also closely related to the Morgan family. When war broke out, Jack and Myfanwy had moved to The Llethrau with their then two youngest children, and left Glenys, their oldest daughter, to help their elderly relations with the farm and housework.

In 1946 they sold Little House to the Craddock family and bought Medwaledd. As soon as Jack and Myfanwy had settled in, they brought their two elderly relations to Medwaledd, along with Glenys, their oldest daughter. By this time Reuben was almost blind, and Jane was nearly 90 years old, but Jack and Myfanwy looked after them well. Then in 1951 Reuben died, and Jane died in 1958 in her 100th year. Both are buried in Felindre Chapel yard.

Now Jack and Myfanwy have more free time to join in the activities of the chapel. Jack had been made a trustee in 1942 and Myfanwy was organist for many years, and also both were good singers and in the Concert Party. The children were also involved in the Sunday School. I can well remember at Harvest Festival time that whilst we would all bring a few flowers or fruit, Myfanwy would always arrive with a tin-bath full of most beautiful blooms. We would be there for hours trying to arrange them and find room for them all in the chapel.

Then, as always happens, the older children got married and moved away; Glenys to Kerry and Mary to Sarn. Then Doug married Margaret Richards, The Lane House, and moved down to Worthen near Shrewsbury. Jack and Myfanwy's youngest daughter Margaret, born at Medwaledd, had married Eric Huffer. Reuben, their youngest son, was never married, so stayed at home with his parents to help with the farming, but soon it became too much hard work, so they sold Medwaledd and bought a house in Newtown and moved there with Reuben. Margaret and Eric stayed on at Medwaledd and worked for Fountain Farmers, who had bought Medwaledd from Jack Mills.

Later, Fountain Farmers sold both The Llethrau and Medwaledd to Tom Harris, The Hendre. Today, one of Tom's workmen, Andrew Gardner, lives at Medwaledd with his wife Karen and children, Ryan and Kara.

Tyn-y-Cwm

This is a large farmhouse just off the Medwaledd Road, and nearly at the top of a steep field. Today it has a good stone road up to the house. Towards the end of the 19th century, the Rev. H.V. Griffiths owned the farm, and also The Ddol.

The Rev. Griffiths was a colonel in the Army and lived in Surrey with his wife and two sons Norman and Denzil, and a daughter. They would come out to Tyn-y-Cwm once a year — I suppose to collect the rent and also have a short holiday. He would always bring a tent and camp out in the meadow with the boys but the ladies would sleep in the house. When they grew up, both boys made their home in America. There was also another little house below Tyn-y-Cwm down by the Rhyddir Brook, called Perks Rhoss, but it is only a few stones and a plum tree today.

In the 1891 census we find Thomas Whittall 59, a farmer, his wife Mary 57, and their children Elizabeth 33, Thomas 26, and William 22, living there. Then by 1901 Thomas was still there with his son Thomas, and young Thomas's wife, Mary 30, along with William Pryce 32, a servant. It is interesting to see that the children did not have to leave home as soon as they left school, as did the children in their little *ty-un-nos* homes on the hills. Their parents were farmers and could afford to keep them at home to work.

I do not know where this Whittall family went to from Tyn-y-Cwm, but the next family I have heard about in connection with the place are the Wildings, The Ddol. Pryce Stephen Wilding married Elizabeth Reynolds, Pencwm, Llaithddu, and they went to Tyn-y-Cwm with Bert, Stephen's brother, who was never married. Elizabeth,

Tyn-y-Cwm. At the moment it is empty

before she was married, was a dressmaker at George Lewis & Sons, London House, Newtown, to where she used to cycle every day. They had three daughters, Joan, Iris and Mary, but Elizabeth was never a strong lady and died in 1939 when the girls were still young — and she was only 39. She is buried in Felindre Baptist yard.

With the coming of the Second World War, many changes were forced upon us, although living out in these hilly, rural areas as we were, life was not nearly as hard as for the city-dwellers. We had our own milk, butter, eggs, vegetables, and potatoes and there were plenty of rabbits to catch, and for Sundays we could have a chicken or cockerel now and again, although they made very good money to dress and sell. Even so, everyone out in the country of working age had to be employed in work deemed useful to help win the war. Farmers were asked to plough more fields, and around these hilly areas, plant potatoes. Acres of potatoes were grown at The Llethrau and Medwaledd, as is mentioned in the history of those farms. Lads who were not needed on the farms had to join the Army, and some did not return. Women also, if they did not have young children, had to join the Forces, the Women's Land Army, or go to work in factories making ammunition for the war. Blodwyn Brick worked in a factory

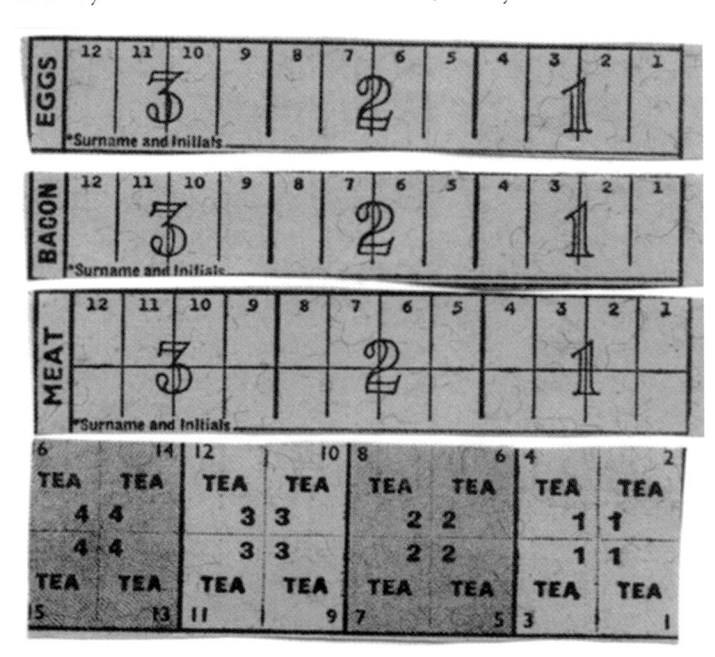

Just imagine having to count all these small coupons at the end of a long, hard day in the shop, and most probably a poor light with which to work

in Newtown, and cycled to Newtown from Nantmel every Monday morning and back Friday night.

At Tyn-y-Cwm, both Pryce and Bert were allowed to stay home and farm and, of course, they had to plant acres of potatoes. It was the same at my home. Before the war, my dad used to give us a short stick — about eighteen inches long — to measure the distance between each potato we planted, but during the war the stick was a good yard or more long, so we soon planted our allocated acreage of land! Shame on us — and we were all Baptists.

Joan was allowed to stay home to look after Pryce and Bert, and also Mary who was still in school, but Iris had to go out to work. She came to the Stores here in the village, which was a very busy place. Mr. Prest, who by then was keeping the shop, had managed to get a licence to sell white petrol, and there were very few pumps around for which this licence was given. This white petrol was only to be used by certain people — doctors, nurses, vets and for some lorries carrying food or important goods needed for the war. Other folk, including farmers, were issued with red petrol coupons, but if they needed to take a sheep to the vet, they could have a small amount of white petrol on their red coupons. My sister was married just after the war had come to an end, but petrol was still rationed; it was amazing how many sheep needed to be taken to the vet that day — and they all had a rest in the Severn Arms Hotel car park. If they were stopped on the way home, they were all just going or coming home from the vet — and in their Sunday best too!

Iris says that folk from far and near would be calling for this white petrol, and handing in their coupons. Then, when the shop closed at night, all these coupons had to be counted, and also the coupons for bread, butter, tea, sugar, eggs, bacon and sweets. As we can see from the ration book below, rationing continued right up until 1954. Bread, marmalade, syrup and treacle were the first items to be de-rationed and the last was meat. At our house, it was sugar that hit us the most, and all five of us children gave it up in our tea so that mum and dad could still have a sweet cup of tea. I have not taken sugar in tea ever since.

Iris with two of her wonderful tapestries

After the war had come to an end, and things were beginning to get back to normal, Iris left the shop and married Ivor Reynolds, The Vron. They first went to live at Lower House, then they moved back to The Vron when Ivor's father built Bankfield and moved there. Ivor has lived at The Vron for 79 years out of his 84 years. He was in the Home Guard during the war, and had many interesting stories to tell. He farmed at The Vron for many years but his pride and joy was his pedigree Hereford bulls. Iris followed in her mother's footsteps to become a very fine needlewoman and has made some wonderful tapestries, and is still working on new ones.

Joan later married Pryce Jones of Kerry and they have two children, Rachael and Thomas, and farm at Old

Bert Wilding

Richard George, Betty George, Gilbert George (The Moat), Hannah Meredith and Mary Wilding. This photograph was taken in the Baptist Chapel where Mary was the organist since she was 13 — a total of 57 years

House, Kerry. Mary never married, but stayed at home and looked after her dad and uncle Bert. She learned to play the piano and passed many exams, even travelling to London or Birmingham to take some of them. She was a beautiful player and could have had work almost anywhere, but she chose to stay at home with family and friends, and where she was needed. Mary was the organist at Felindre Baptist Chapel since she was 13 years old — a total of fifty-seven years. She would also come to Cwmgwyn to play on Anniversary day, when John Stephens would be conducting the choir. Mary and John would have been first cousins.

Doug, my husband, used to take Mary's bread and a few groceries up to Tyn-y-Cwm for her most weeks, as she could not drive. She would always want him to come in and sing and she would play the piano. One day, she rang up her sister Joan and in her lovely old-fashioned way of talking, told her sister to 'harken here now'. She put the 'phone down on a table by the piano, and away they went, singing and playing and Joan listening on the other end of the 'phone. Most probably it was a good old Sankey hymn.

There was always a welcome at Tyn-y-Cwm, especially for the local roadmen who would call in if they were working anywhere near. They would hide their shovels if it was still in working time, and Tom James of Fiddlers Green and Jack Price of Cork Hall have enjoyed many a game of dominoes, Ludo or fox-and-geese at Tyn-y-Cwm.

The house has never been modernized, but Mary did have the telephone put in many years ago. She was afraid of it, if there was thunder and lightning about, but otherwise she used and enjoyed it. Mary always dressed very smartly in expensive clothes, and always wore a fine hat to come to chapel, but her means of transport in later years was in the transport box with uncle Bert driving the tractor. Bert died in 1978 aged 79 and is buried in Felindre Baptist Chapel yard. After that, her good friend Clifford Goodman used to go up to collect her, bringing her down to chapel in his old black car.

Mary died in 1999, never having visited the doctor for sixty years, and never having lived in another house. She is buried in Felindre Chapel yard, and has donated money for new oak doors on the entrance to the chapel. Mary will be sorely missed by many.

Tyn-y-Cwm is now empty, but her nephew, Thomas, farms the land. The house is structurally sound and, I feel, when it has been modernized will make a lovely and happy home for a family.

The lost homes on Cilvaesty Hill

High Park

This is a little house up on Cilvaesty Hill, and the first dwelling reached when going up from the chapel. There is a very steep rough road up the hill, then it is out a little way on the open hill.

In the 1891 census an Edward Jones 32 farmer, and his sister Margaret 31, lived there, and both were still there in the 1901 census. Later, they both moved to the pub in Beguildy which locally was called 'The Thatchings' because, I suppose, of its thatched roof.

Then came some of the Lloyd family, and there were several Lloyds living up on the hills around The Llethrau. A Mr. W. Lloyd, High Park, was on the Building Committee of Cwmgwyn Chapel in the early years of it being Baptist. A Mary (Polly) Lloyd married Jack Hamer from Mochdre, and they came to live at High Park. This couple had six children — Mildred, May, Elsie, Beattie, Tom and Noel. Mildred went to live down near Kington. May married Hector Morgan, and they lived at Amblecote. Hector was tragically killed when a horse kicked him and punctured his lung. They had one son, Celwyn, who lives in Newtown and, I think, is still a bus driver. Elsie married John George, and they farmed at Penarron, Kerry, and she was a member of Cwmgwyn Chapel, as indeed, were most of the Hamer

Mr. and Mrs. Hamer with their children

High Park is still standing but is now empty. Here, Elsie, John and young Stephen are seen standing outside

family. Many years ago, I used to drive over to Kerry once a month to collect our preacher, the Rev. L.M. Richards, and would often pick up Elsie on my way and bring her back to the service. Beattie married Ben Evans and lived at Cwmdolfa, Kerry. George Davies's wife, Lily Evans, was a sister to Ben.

Tom Hamer never married. He used to work at farms around in the area and says he came to help Doug at the Waen when we first moved there, there was certainly plenty of work needed doing at the Waen at that time, I can tell you. In later life, Tom started investing his money in property. He bought his home, High Park, Panty-Beudy and Tynllwyn, where he lived and farmed. When the farming became too hard a job, Tom bought a house in Newtown and his nephew, Stephen George, a son of Elsie, farmed Tynllwyn, but let the house to David and Jane Penlington. Tom now lives in a little bungalow in Newtown.

Noel was the youngest, and like Tom, never married. Noel worked on the road and, oh how we miss our roadmen these days. There would be no great pools of water lying on the road for days — the drains would always be kept open. Also there would be no dead foxes and badgers left on the roads for weeks. Noel lived in a caravan near the Hendy and kept several cats. When he retired, he moved to a house in Kerry where he died in 2002, aged 69. He is buried in Felindre yard, near to his parents.

Both Jack and Polly were regular attendees at Cwmgwyn Chapel, and Jack was made a trustee in 1942. The first year we were at the Waen, I climbed up that very steep hill, pushing David in the pushchair, and went to High Park to see Mrs. Hamer and have a rest. She would always have a cup of tea and a piece of fruit cake ready in no time. I remember the fruit cake was kept in a basket hanging from the ceiling.

I would then go out on the hill and pick a few whimberries. They were not very plentiful as so many sheep were kept on the open hill. In the 1920s and '30s whole families would go out picking whimberries and sell them to help pay the rent. I can remember my dad and mum taking all five of us up the hill and they took the tin bath to put the whimberries in. They were a good cheap source of money back in those days, but there was a lot of work even after we had picked them. They had to be cleaned of all the little green leaves and stalks, then carried to town, or to meet trains to be taken to town.

In about 1940, when the Second World War had just started, we were offered a very good price for whimberries. Apparently they were used to dye the Royal Air Force uniforms, and we were paid four shillings per pound. That was about four times the amount we had been getting before, so we were up on that hill as often as possible — and we did not have to clean them.

Thinking back to High Park, I can remember a most beautiful red geranium, which just about filled the window, and the open fire with a pit in the floor just a little way out in the room. This would hold the ashes for several days.

Although High Park was only a little house with two bedrooms, I have heard that at one time there were ten people living there. Two of these ten were the parents of Jack or Polly. Often the children would look after their parents, as the workhouse would have been the only other alternative for them.

Jack died in 1959 aged 72, and Polly died in 1963 aged 76. Both are buried in Felindre Baptist yard.

Slate House

This was yet another little house built out on Cilvaesty Hill. In 1891 we find a Richard Jones 66, farmer, living there with his wife Elizabeth 58, daughters Martha 22, and Mary Anne 12, mother-in-law Martha Whittall 76, a granddaughter Anne Davies 2, along with a servant, John Evans 73, and a labourer, John Jones 20.

By 1901 only Richard and Elizabeth are still there, but with Edwin Lewis 22, a servant. In those days, the children had to go out to work as soon as they left school and could find a job.

The next family we hear about were the Pughs. George Pugh and his wife Annie moved there in 1919, and I have been very fortunate to talk to one of their grandchildren — Mrs. Dorothy Gough, now living in Newcastle, who used to spend her holidays up at Slate House, and loved to be there. It was always a happy home, with lots of people calling, and a warm welcome for all.

George and Annie Pugh had five children — Gilbert, whom we hear quite a lot about in the history of Cwmgwyn Chapel, then Tommy and Pryce (who were twins), Mary and Lily. Mary went to keep house for a Henry Jones, a relation of Cecil Lloyd and his father, and they had 'let' Medwaledd to him. While there, Mary

George and Annie Pugh with their five children: Mary, twin boys Tommy and Pryce, Gilbert (centre) and Lily

and Henry were married, and Dorothy Gough is their daughter. Lily, the youngest, married a Meredith from Llanbadarn, and one of their sons is Sydney Meredith, Trebrodier, Beguildy.

Dorothy remembers singing the old Sankey hymns while up at Slate House, with Lily playing the organ. She used to thoroughly enjoy these singsong evenings. Once she remembers some folk coming up from South Wales, probably some distant relatives who had left the area years before and had gone to work in the coalmines. They knew there would be a warm welcome at Slate House, with good food and good singing, and I suppose it would be like a holiday for them. Dorothy thinks there were only three bedrooms, but there was always room for everyone.

Maggie Pugh, who was always working in different homes looking after the sick, or helping out when a new baby arrived, was at one time very poorly herself. She went to Slate House to be looked after and nursed back to health. She was of the same Pugh family as George Pugh, and I think Mrs. Blodwyn Brick, who was a Pugh before she married Arthur, was also of the same Pugh family.

Dorothy remembers that during a dry spell when the water would be in short supply up at the house, they would load up all their clothes needing washing and the boiler onto the cart, and head down the hill to the River Teme to wash. They would collect a few sticks and light a fire under the boiler to boil all the whites, and then they would have good hot water to wash all the coloured clothes, and lastly the working clothes and socks. All the clothes were put in the river to rinse, and loaded back up on the cart to take home to dry and iron.

What a wonderful gift is water, and another free gift is wind. Les Morris, who kept the Wharf Inn many years ago, set up a windmill in the garden which would generate enough electricity to have electric lights in the pub, and the new folk at Butterwell have wind-powered electricity for lights and also to drive a pump to get the water from the well into the house. Also in the history of Gwenlas, we read about John Davies and his water-powered electricity.

Dorothy has also told me about four brothers from the Kerry area who were her great-uncles. Mr. Meredith Thomas, who owned The Stores here in Felindre, had taken these boys as apprentice 'store keepers', and his rules were that each boy should serve four years, during which time they would live and sleep at The Stores. This meant that there was a Jones boy at The Stores over a period of sixteen years altogether. I wonder how many of our teenage boys today would be willing to do that, but in those days they would have had a warm house and bed, with good food and a small amount of pocket money as well.

Later in life, Dorothy says that Ernest emigrated to Canada, where he later owned his own farm; Harry ran his own store in Llangollen, North Wales; Tom worked in a high-class gents' outfitters in Bridgnorth; and Richard ran a general stores, firstly in Sarn, then in Kerry, and would deliver goods and groceries around the houses and farms with a horse and cart — just as Meredith Thomas used to do around Felindre. It sounds as if their apprenticeship paid dividends in the long run.

The Pugh family moved away in about 1946, and there has been no one living at Slate House since. The house is now down and only a few stones remain — along with many happy memories.

The Lluest

This was a small homestead on Cilvaesty hill, but today it is only a shed and a row of fir trees around, which can easily be seen from the front window of the chapel. It was recorded 'empty' in both the 1891 and 1901 census forms, and the only information I could find was that the older folk around here remembered the people who used to live further out on the hill, and that they would all meet up at The Lluest gate on a Sunday evening and walk down the hill to chapel together.

In 2004 I had a 'phone call from a Joyce Davies who used to live at Dolfrynog. She says that she has now heard of news of her great-great-grandparents, who were the last people to live at The Lluest. They were Elizabeth and James Davies.

In 1841 this James Davies was a servant lad at Cwmgwyn Hall for the Francis family. Then in 1851 he moved to The Lluest and was recorded as a 'farmer of twelve acres'. Elizabeth was born in Aberhafesp in 1832 to Thomas and Elizabeth Pryce. When she was 9 years old the family moved to Dolfrynog, then when she left school she went to work as housekeeper for James Davies at The Lluest. In 1855 they were married and George Francis, Cwmgwyn Hall, was their witness.

In 1861 we find this couple had moved from The Lluest to Windy Hall, and by 1881 they were living at Dolfrynog, which in those days was often called 'The Little Ddol'. They were still there in 1891, James now 92, and Elizabeth 69, and with them were their grandchildren, Maurice and George.

Joyce has sent two cuttings from the *Montgomery Express and Radnor Times*. The first was dated June 25th and headed 'Serious Accident', and gives

James and Elizabeth Davies, the last couple to live at The Lluest

a lengthy and detailed account of an accident in which Elizabeth was involved. The second report a week later is headed 'Fatal Accident at Newtown', and again is lengthy and detailed, and also a very sad story:

> FATAL ACCIDENT AT NEWTOWN — An inquest was held at the Infirmary, Newtown on Thursday evening by the Coroner (Mr. Richard Williams) and a jury of which Mr. Jno. Swain was foreman, to enquire into the death of Elizabeth Davies, Cwmgwyn, Beguildy, who died at the Infirmary on the previous night as the result of injuries sustained in an accident on the Dolfor-road the previous Tuesday week, the facts of which we reported in our last issue.
>
> Maurice Davies, Little Ddol, Cwmgwyn, Beguildy said he was a farmer, and the deceased, who was his grandmother, was 70 years of age. About 6 o'clock in the evening of Tuesday the 18th inst. he was returning home from Newtown market with a cart drawn by two horses and he led the shaft horse. The deceased was in the cart, which also contained two 18 gallon barrels of

beer, half a sack of flour, half a sack of corn, and two half sacks of meal with several baskets and parcels. Everything went all right until they got to the second lamp post on the Dolfor-road, when the horses took fright at something and witness lost his hold of the shaft horse and they galloped for nearly 200 yards. When they came to the culvert crossing the brook at the entrance to the Plantation-lane, the cart came into collision with the parapet on the Dolfor side of the culvert and the right wheel broke. Deceased was thrown into the road, while the barrels rolled into the brook. From the lamp post to the culvert there was no protection to prevent anyone or anything falling into the brook, which was two or three feet below the surface of the road. Witness overtook the cart in a few seconds and went to the assistance of the deceased. He saw the wheel pass over her, but none of the contents of the cart fell upon her. A woman assisted his grandmother and he attended to the horses, which he took to the Sportsman Inn. A doctor was summoned, and the police conveyed deceased to the Infirmary on an ambulance. When on the ground, deceased groaned and seemed to be in great pain.

Dr. Alfred Shearer said he acted as Dr. Purchas' assistant. About 6 o'clock in the evening of the 18th inst. he was called to the Dolfor-road. He went at once and found the deceased lying on her back on some sacks against the parapet wall of a culvert. On a slight examination he found her suffering severely from shock and she complained of great pain in her left hip-joint. He summoned the ambulance and under his superintendence she was conveyed to the Infirmary. There he made a careful examination and found both knees and one hand cut, while the pelvis was fractured. There were severe bruises on the lower part of the abdomen and on both thighs, and a small bruise under the left eye. No bone was broken except the pelvis. There was no external bleeding except a little in the lower part of the abdomen and no indications of internal injury as far as he could discover. As soon as she arrived at the Infirmary, he gave her a dose of strychnine and brandy to allay the shock. Then Dr. Raywood and himself bandaged her and applied other remedies.

Witness attended her to the time of her death. The injuries to the abdomen and pelvis appeared to have been caused by a wheel passing over that part of the body. Deceased had recovered well from the shock by the Friday following, but on the Monday bronchitis set in, which proved fatal. Bronchitis was often the result of an accident of this kind to a person of deceased's age. The immediate cause of death was bronchitis, brought on as a direct result of the accident.

Mrs. Elizabeth Evans, 13 Frankwell Street, Newtown said she was coming down the Dolfor-road on the evening in question when she saw two horses drawing a cart coming towards her at full gallop. Deceased was in the cart, and when witness attempted to stop the horses, she cried "let them go". Witness crossed the culvert into the Plantation-lane for safety. The horses swerved towards the Cefnaire fence and then back again to the wall of the culvert, with which the cart collided. Deceased was jerked into the road and some barrels were thrown into the brook. Witness ran to the deceased and found her lying under the left wheel of the cart, which rested partly on her back and partly on her left side. She could not get deceased from under the wheel until the other wheel broke. Deceased said, "Let me alone; I am dying." Witness assisted her to get up, and she leaned against witness, but requested her to lay her down again. Deceased said her hip and back were broken. Witness believed that Maurice Davies, who was leading the horses, was perfectly sober.

Miss Alice Emma Kinsey, Dingle Farm, near Newtown said she witnessed the accident and attended to the deceased with the last witness. She fetched Dr. Shearer and the police.

Robert Owen, groom, Belle Vue, Newtown said he saw Maurice Davies do his best to stop the horses bolting, but he was obliged to let go. Witness saw the cart collide with the wall and the wheel pass over the deceased.

Miss Margaret Jenkins, nurse at the Infirmary, said she attended the deceased from the date of her admission to the time of her death, which took place at ten minutes to twelve on the night of the 26th inst. The windows were never open at nights, but were sometimes during the day. A screen was always placed to keep the draught from the deceased.

The Coroner having summed up, the Jury returned a verdict in accordance with the medical evidence, and "desired to call the attention of the County Council and the Newtown members of it to the dangerous and unprotected state of the road at the place where the accident took place".

Persandy

They say there are two Persandy houses quite near to each other, so perhaps as sometimes happens, a new house was built there and the old one kept as shelter for the animals in winter.

In the 1891 census we find a Mary Jones 69, as the head of the household consisting of Hannah Jones 23, her daughter, and Jane 1, a granddaughter, along with Percival Hughes, a nursing child and Samuel Jones, a labourer. By 1901 Hannah is the head and shares the house with Jane, her daughter, who is now 11, and Richard Jenkins, a labourer.

Dorothy Gough, a granddaughter for George and Annie Pugh, Slate House, thinks that some time later Mr. Mytton Davies from Berriew, who owned Slate House, bought Persandy and used to let it out to tenants from time to time. Then in 1939–40, when the war had started, Mr. John Lloyd and his son Cecil were asked to leave The Llethrau, and they went to Persandy and farmed there (while the war was on). I think the Lloyds were reluctant to plough up some of their land and plant potatoes, so The Llethrau was commandeered by the Ministry of Defence, and Mr. Jack Mills moved there from Little House and was put in charge of lorryloads of prisoners of war, firstly Italian men, then Germans. After the war, Mr. Jack Mills moved to Medwaledd, and Cecil moved back to The Llethrau, but I think his father, John Lloyd, had died just before, at the age of 81. He was buried in Crug-y-Byddar Church yard with his wife Mary, who had died in 1920 aged 48, and Marsh, a son who died in 1923 aged 30. Cecil died in 1963 aged 63 and all four Lloyds are recorded on the same headstone in Crug-y-Byddar Church yard.

The Lloyds were the last people to live at Persandy.

The Anchor Road

The Turgey

This is a farmhouse just along the Anchor road on the left hand side as going from the Gorther. It was a very old house even on the turn of the century, and had a stone-tiled roof with very strong supporting beams. It also had a waterwheel for driving some of the farm machinery.

In the 1891 census a Henry Hamer 21, lived there with Mary Brown 31, his housekeeper, and Martin Cadwallader 13, a servant boy. By 1901 Henry Hamer had moved to The Oaks, which is just further along the Anchor road on the right-hand side, and a Mr. Edward Davies 33, his wife Jane 34, and their young son Sidney, moved into The Turgey. This little family had come up from the coalmines in South Wales and were going to live at The Waen, but the new house was not finished, so in the meantime they went to live at The Turgey. Edward was a Mochdre man and Jane was a Thomas, the Criggin, Llanbister. Jane would have been a cousin to Doug Thomas, my husband. Whilst at The Turgey, Millie and the twin boys, Edward and Vincent, were born.

Later, we hear of Arthur Pugh — the youngest son of James and Eliza Pugh, Medwaledd — moving to The Turgey with his wife, Margaret Jane, from Bryndrinog, Newcastle. While at The Turgey they had two children, Ethel and Arthur. These children attended Crug-y-Byddar School and Felindre Baptist Chapel. Richard Williams of Walk Mill, in his letter to me, says they all walked together to Felindre Chapel, come rain or shine.

In 1926 Arthur and Margaret left The Turgey and moved to The Oaks. I think this Pugh family was the last to live at The Turgey, and the house is now mostly in ruins, although there is a shed still being used. The Pugh family now farm the land together with The Oaks.

The Oaks

This is another farmhouse on the right hand side of the Anchor road just along from The Turgey. In the 1891 census a Richard Pryce 49, a farmer, and his wife Mary 43, and their children, William 13, Anne 9, and Jane 6, lived there. Richard and Mary were still there in 1901 together with daughter Jane. The other two children had obviously found work elsewhere.

I think the next people to live at The Oaks were Henry Hamer and his housekeeper Mary Brown, who had lived with him before at The Turgey.

Some time later Henry and his housekeeper moved again, this time to Rhyddir Oak, and Mrs. Mary Anne Reynolds moved to The Oaks. Mary Anne had moved up from the coalmines in South Wales with her brother, Thomas James. Thomas married Laura Jane Morgan and lived at Fiddlers Green, and Mary Anne married a Sam Reynolds and they lived at The Oaks. Mary and Sam had three daughters — Jane, Irene and Ruby — and they later moved down to the Criggin

Cottage in Felindre. Irene and Ruby married the twin boys from The Waen — Edward and Vincent — and Jane married Ernie Jones from Llanbadarn. Their mother, who by then was a widow, married a Nicholls and continued to live in the village. Ruby and her mother are both buried in Felindre Baptist yard, also Ruby's husband Vincent, and their son John.

The Oaks with snowdrops on the lawn

In 1926 Arthur and Margaret Pugh moved from The Turgey to The Oaks with their two children, Ethel and Arthur, and later Stanley was born. This family continued to work both farms together. Ethel married Hubert Roberts from the Church House, Bettws, and went to live at the Travelly. Arthur and Stanley continued to live at The Oaks with their parents, then their mother died in 1960 aged 65 and their father died in 1976 aged 88.

Stanley can remember his dad telling him about a young man and his housekeeper living at The Oaks, and one year she planted hundreds of snowdrop bulbs in the lawn, which still flower year by year. This would have been Henry Hamer and the housekeeper, Mary Brown. Stanley has given me a photograph of the house with the snowdrops in flower.

Mr. and Mrs. Pugh moved from The Turgey to The Oaks in 1926

Arthur used to come down to our shop on a Saturday morning for the local paper, a pint of milk and some dried peas, ready to cook for next day. These peas were put to soak overnight with a little bi-carb. This was before tinned or frozen peas came about, and these were the only peas I can remember when I was young.

Then in 1990 Arthur died and was buried in Felindre Baptist yard with his parents. Stanley continues to live at The Oaks by himself, although I think his sister Ethel and her children come over to see him quite often.

Newcwm

In the 1891 census an Aaron Botwood 42, farmer, his wife Mary 42, and their children, William 13, Anne 9 and Jane 6, lived at Newcwm. Then by 1901 a William Morris 38, a roadman, and his wife Jane 37, and their children, Elizabeth 22, John 10 and Jane 7 lived there, but I know no more about the Morris family.

However, Clarence and Muriel Botwood live at Gwrid Farm near the Anchor, and they tell me about Teddy Botwood who lived at The Nanty and came to Denmark with our Dolithon choir. Another relation is the Rev. Tudor Botwood, who has preached in Cwmgwyn Chapel at more than one Harvest Festival. When the war in Iraq first started, Tudor joined the Navy and was chaplain on the *Ark Royal*. This ship was involved in the rescuing of our pilots when two of their planes were shot down over the sea. Tudor was awarded the British Empire Medal by the Queen for his services. He is still in the Navy and is based in Portsmouth.

The first person that anyone today remembers living at Newcwm was George Webster and his wife and their son Lesley, which was in the early 1930s. George worked on the forestry and Lesley, who now lives in Bucknell, has told me a little

The Williams family, Newcwm.
From left to right. Standing: Linda, Bob, Olwen, Vida, Richard and Tilda.
Seated: Jinny, Mrs. Williams (a daughter for Charlie [the Prysg]), Mr. Williams (a son for Elizabeth [Yrchen]), Patty

about Newcwm, which was a smallholding owned by John Lloyd and his son Cecil, The Llethrau. The Websters rented this holding from the Lloyds for £12 per year, so with his job on the forestry they could have had a reasonable living, with poultry, pigs and maybe a milking cow on the land.

Lesley remembers going to Crug-y-Byddar School and when he first started, Arthur and Stanley, The Oaks, used to look after him. Lesley thinks they left Newcwm about the end of 1939 to 1940, moving to Holly Farm in the Stanage area. He can remember that on the day they moved, the Williams family were in the yard waiting to take their place, while they were still loading their belongings onto the wagon.

Alice and Jim Williams had started their married life at Walk Mill — a smallholding just above the Gorther. Their first child, Richard, was born at Walk Mill. Alice was a daughter for Charlie Morgan, The Prysg, and Jim was a son from Yrchen, so they did not move very far in those days. This family next moved to Newhouse, or The Nest, which has now been bought by Paul Barrett who has been very busy repairing and renovating it for the past couple of years, as well as continuing his normal work.

Alice and Jim had six more children while living at The Nest — Tilda, Olwen, Patty, Vida, Bob and Linda. Jim worked at Tyndol for Mr. Thomas, as a farm labourer.

Here is a lovely letter I had from Richard, when I wrote and asked him for a history of his family:

Dear Mrs. Thomas,

This is Dick Williams, eldest son of James and Alice Williams of Newcwm Farm, Felindre. I was born at a little holding called The Walk Mill. When I came to school age, I attended Crug-y-Byddar School. We had very good neighbours. On our right were Mr. and Mrs. Reynolds, the Vron, and on our left, Mr. and Mrs. Davies, The Gorther. Not forgetting Mr. and Mrs. Wilding, Tyn-y-Cwm and Mr. and Mrs. Pugh, The Oaks, who walked with us to the Baptist Chapel — whatever the weather. At the time, Dad worked for Mr. Reynolds, Rhyd-y-Cwm.

As time went on, we moved to Newhouse or The Nest as some people called it, where Dad worked for Mr. Owen Thomas, Tyndol. On leaving school, I joined him for two years when we were very happy working together in the Felindre Happy Valley, where we all knew one another.

After that, I moved down country to the Whitton area, where I met my wife, Agnes Meredith. We worked on different farms around there. I was alright down there, but it was not Felindre Valley, where I had grown up.

Anyhow, in 1939 we decided to get married. As it happened, my wife Agnes was housekeeper for Mr. Davies, Gwernerrin, so we met in Felindre Baptist every Sunday. That gave Agnes the chance to meet the people and to get used to the Felindre Valley, where she was happy to be.

It had come time for Dad to take things a bit easier. He heard of Newcwm holding to let and got it. Then, he wanted me to take his job on at Tyndol, so between Dad and Mr. Thomas, I took it on with a struggle to get £2 a week — not the £200 as it is now. But we were happy in the Felindre Valley, until the war came in 1940, and Mr. Thomas, Tyndol gave up the farm, and I left the old Felindre Valley.

With much regret.

Pryce R[ichard]. Williams

Tilda Williams and Albert Price on their Ruby Wedding anniversary, which they celebrated at The Lamb, Kerry

Well, it sounds as if Richard loved living in the Valley, and I have actually heard this from other folk. It was such a busy and yet very caring valley, with some very large families and some very hardworking people living in it.

When most of the Williams children had married and moved away, Tilda and her husband, Albert Price, remained at Newcwm. They were both good singers and Albert, or Ab, was a very good chairman and was often in demand at concerts. They were always in

Newcwm as it is today. The original part is that built in stone to the left, the rendered addition being added by the Brown family

the Cwmgwyn Concert Party and later both were in the Dolithon Choir with Ab as our compère. They had a son, David, who is now an assistant headmaster in a school in North Wales.

Albert worked on the forestry, and kept the smallholding of Newcwm. When he retired, they left Newcwm and moved to Penlan, just outside Kerry. Later, Ab died and Tilda Price moved into the village of Kerry, where she still lives.

By the 1950s, the Browns lived at Newcwm, and they doubled the size of the house by building the two-storey addition, and also some wooden stables.

Ron and Judy Horne lived at Newcwm until November 1995. They further added to the house, built more block stables, and opened access directly from the lane instead of from the Common.

The lady now living at Newcwm is Mrs. Gomm. She has three daughters — Nancy, who has married Richard Adams and lives nearby at Anchorage Cottage; one daughter who lives in America; and one daughter who lives near Dorchester, Dorset. One of Mrs. Gomm's granddaughters was married in Bettws Church in 2004.

This is a very old church and a lovely setting for a wedding. It was built many centuries ago on a lonely and windswept hillside on the side of an old drovers' road. Indeed, standing at 1,300 feet above sea level it is said to be the highest church in England. The first worshippers would probably have been hill shepherds and drovers, but over the years the building has had a wealth of history and interesting people involved in it. I have heard that the very last hurdy-gurdy, or barrel organ, to be used in a church was here in Bettws Church — but now they have a modern electric organ.

The marriage of Mrs. Gomm's granddaughter at Bettws-y-Crwyn

The Trefoil Hill

Hope's Castle

This is another of our little clod houses, with a rather grand name. I wonder if this was because, when they had finished their little house within the time limit and saw the first smoke coming out of the chimney before sunrise, to them it was their 'castle'. I have also heard of The Palace out on Maelienydd, Windy Hall up near Cwmgwyn and Cork Hall near Little House.

In the 1891 census a John Williams aged 61, and his wife Sarah 65, lived and farmed there, together with Edward Harding aged 30, a labourer. These three were still there in 1901.

I know no more about John and Sarah Williams, but Edward Harding, or Ned as he was known, was a wisket and basket maker, selling them at half-a-crown each. A wisket was similar to a basket but much larger and oval-shaped with a handle at each end. Both these items would have been widely used in those days, so Ned would have been kept quite busy. Some days he would walk up to the Llanbadarn road by Butterwell so as to catch the people walking back home from Newtown, being able to both take orders and deliver those already ordered.

I can remember using a wisket to carry food to the cattle kept indoors in the winter. The food would be pulped swedes mixed with chaff, both of which we would have prepared that evening, the swedes brought in from the tump in the rick-yard, and put through the pulper, turning the handle by hand, whilst the chaff was straw which had been cut into small pieces by putting it through the chaff-cutter. This machine would be driven by a horse walking round and round outside at the horse-works, which would drive a belt and provide power to the chaff-cutter

Hope's Castle, with the road passing beyond the house and joining the main road just above Little House Lane. It was called the Red Road, but today is impassable

in the barn. The chaff would then be mixed with the pulped swede and fed to the cattle.

Ned later moved to The Slopes, but still kept making his baskets and wiskets. However, at the age of 73, Ned was found dead up by The Oaks in January 1930, after a heavy snowstorm. Arthur Brick and the local policeman managed to get Arthur's lorry up to The Oaks, and brought him home. He is buried in Crug-y-Byddar Church yard.

The next people we hear about living at Hope's Castle are the Lloyds — and there were many Lloyds living up around the Cwmgwyn area. This was Bill Lloyd, a brother to the Lloyds at the Rhuvid.

Later, Bill Goodman farmed there for about four years, and then the Richards family moved in and are still there today. Frank Richards, who was brought up with Jo Richards at Shell Heath, married Eleanor Pryce from the Lane House. They both worked for Tom Harris, the Hendre, and when this Tom Harris moved to Aston-on-Clun, they both moved with him. Later they came back up to this area, firstly to Tack Barn, Beguildy, then to Llanmadog, and then they settled at Hope's Castle. They had seven children — Olive, Molly, Frank, John, Austin, Edgar and Rowena.

During the last war, Mr. and Mrs. Richards moved to Medwaledd with Rowena, and John stayed on at Hope's Castle to farm. While at Medwaledd, they worked for

Left: Mr. and Mrs. Frank Richards with, right, their son, also Frank, who was the school caretaker for many years

Maureen, Sandra and Craig Richards

Edgar Richards

the Ministry of Defence and had Italian prisoners-of-war to work on the farm. As with The Llethrau, it was mostly growing potatoes.

John Richards had stayed on at Hope's Castle and is still there. He married Olwen Pugh from Cwm-Jenkins and they had three children, Maureen, Sandra and Craig. The two girls used to come to Sunday School at Cwmgwyn, and they would recite and sing on the Anniversary Day. They both married and moved away, but Craig still lives at home with his dad, and works for Chris Thomas, Bryndraenog, on the farm.

Olwen was a great walker, and loved to walk the long distance footpaths such as Glyndwr's Way and, with her friend Alma Lewis, she once walked Hadrian's Wall. One of the greatest Roman rulers, Hadrian, had this wall built in A.D. 121 from Newcastle to Carlisle, for the protection of his lands against the Scots — and I would think that to have Hadrian's Wall 'under your belt' would be a great achievement. Sadly, Olwen died in 1994 at the age of 62 and is buried in Felindre Chapel yard. Maureen's husband sadly died in 1997 at the age of 49. He was from the Llanidloes area and is buried next to Olwen.

Later Mr. and Mrs. Richards moved from Medwaledd to the Old Post Office next to the Manse in Felindre. George and Barbara Barrett live there now. Then after the war had been won, the Council built Felindre's 'Victory Houses'. An Aaron Bright was the first to live in No. 2 house, followed by Robin Hall for a short while, and then Mr. and Mrs. Richards who lived there for many years. They always kept a good vegetable garden, and also some lovely old-fashioned flowers, one year gaining second place in the local council house best kept gardens competition. Austin, their son, lives there now, and again he keeps the garden in good shape.

Eleanor Richards died in 1972 aged 80, and Frank died in 1973 aged 82. Both are buried in the Felindre Baptist yard.

And so Hope's Castle is one of the few clod houses to have been used as a farmhouse right through the century. The fact that it has a good solid road right up to the house could be one of the reasons and, of course, the same family has lived in it now for well over sixty years.

These next seven little dwellings out on the Trefoil Hill are now all gone, with very little trace of the houses — just memories — and those nearly forgotten!!

The Bog

This was another little clod house out on the open hill just beyond Hope's Castle and Brickhouse. As the name implies, it was a wet, boggy patch of ground and the farmers around would be pleased to see these wet patches fenced in, so would encourage and help the farm worker to build his house. When the land was fenced in the farmer's sheep could not graze there and so, hopefully, not get the harmful fluke-worm that could often prove fatal.

In the 1891 census, Richard Harding 39, his wife Anne 34, and their six children, Hannah 11, Richard 10, Robert 8, Elsie 6, John 3, and Minnie 1, lived there, but by 1901 these had all moved away and a Mary Price 59, a widow, and her granddaughter, Harriet Jones, lived there.

Later we hear of Jack Price and his wife, who was Sarah Richards — a daughter for Jo Richards of Shell Heath — living there with their children, Harold, Pryce, Bert, Dick, Jo, Watkin, Nancy (the only girl) and David, the youngest. Sadly Sarah, the mother, died in 1916 after David was born, and is buried in the new yard in Felindre.

The father stayed at home with his daughter after his wife died, but several of the boys were brought up in a children's home in Knighton. Dick had to spend most part of a year in hospital with T.B., then came back to live with Mr. and Mrs. Richards (the parents of Austin Richards of Hope's Castle) for a while. He then went to the home in Knighton where some of his brothers were. He was always a bright and loveable lad, and when the electricity first came to Knighton he was given the honour of switching it on. Dick joined the Territorial Army and trained in the Beacons, and when the Second World War broke out he joined the Army straight away. He fought in Arnhem with one of Austin's brothers-in-law. His specialist role was as a wireless operator for a Commanding Officer.

After the war, he returned to Felindre. His father and Nancy had moved from The Bog to Cork Hall, then to the Lane House. Then together with his father, brother Jo, and sister Nancy, bought Cefn Derw and farmed there, but as it proved hard to make a living in farming, Dick took a job in Knighton as a postman, and soon he was delivering post up the Teme valley. At one time he was also the rent collector for the ground on the open hill. Locally this was known as The King's Rent, and was in lieu of stock kept on the Crown land. It would not amount to much — around here it was only a few shillings per household (less than £1), but in those days was still difficult to find. Quite often the mother and children would pick whimberries to pay the rent. Dick once told me the rules of this job. He had to find, or dig, a hole in the ground, deep enough so that they could not be seen from the road and big enough for two men to stand in. The collecting point where he had to work was up above Maesgwyn, just as you go out on the open hill on the right hand side of the road as if going to Crossway. This tax also allowed the small farmers to cut and store turf for their fires in winter. It was called the Turf and Knife Tax.

When their father died in 1963, Dick, Nancy and Jo sold Cefn Derw and moved to Knucklas. Jo worked on the road and Dick was still posting. After Jo and Nancy had died, Dick built himself a beautiful little bungalow nearly under the viaduct, and enjoyed his new home for several years.

However, age creeps up on us all, and Dick had to move to Stapeley House Nursing Home in Knighton, where he died in 2002 at the age of 88, and is buried next to his parents (Jack had died in 1963), Watkin, who had died on active service in 1942, Nancy and Jo, in Felindre.

Dick was the one of the family I knew best, although I remember Harold when he lived at Dolau. He had a good voice and used to sing duets with Doug. When I first met Dick, he was coming up to The Waen to look after our bees. Our boys used to be fascinated watching him extract the honey, and one time I brought my class up from school to watch.

I think that the Price family were the last to live at The Bog and Cork Hall. Later, the old Mr. Lakelin used to rent The Bog and would use the ground floor of the house as shelter for his animals whilst storing fodder upstairs. I can remember one very stormy night, when the snow was falling thick and fast, the old man knocked us up quite late at night and asked for help. He was going to run his tractor up and down all night to try to keep the road open up to The Bog, and would need fuel for his tractor. It was freezing cold and tractors had no cabs in those days, but he was as hard as nails and kept that road open. He was a remarkable old man.

I think The Bog is mostly in ruins now, so yet another of these little *ty-un-nos* homes is no more, but it had served its purpose well, giving a home and shelter to several families during its lifetime.

Shell Heath

This was a little clod house out on the open hill between Killowent and The Ddol, Llanbadarn. In the 1891 census a Joseph Richards 54, a farmer, his wife Mary 44, and his stepchildren, Anne Owens 10, Pryce Owens 8, Sarah Owens 6, and their daughter Martha Richards aged 3, lived there. Jo Richards also had a family before he married Mary — Jack, Pryce, Annie, Jane and Doris.

By the time of the 1901 census Jo Richards, his wife and daughter Martha, now 13, and also Frank Owens 10, a grandson, had moved to The Trefoil — another little homestead further out on the hill. This was while Shell Heath house was being rebuilt, then they would move back.

This Jo Richards was a grandfather for Frank Richards, the Lane House, who married Frances Marpole. Jo also brought up Austin's (of Hope's Castle) dad, another Frank Richards, but yet more people were living in this little two up / two down house, for Charlie Higgins made his home here with Jo and Mary. Later he lived with his wife Jessie in Dolau and they are both buried in Felindre yard. 'Red' Tom Morgan also lived at Shell Heath and worked for Matthews, Upper House, Felindre. He would walk there for eight o'clock, but if he were a minute late, he would have to work another half hour at night.

With no waterproof clothing, and no wellingtons, I just wonder how on earth they all got their clothes dry by morning, or did they just get back in to them — still wet! When we were living at The Waen, and we had five boys to feed and clothe, I can well remember an advert in the *Farmers' Weekly* for waterproof trousers and jackets for children. What a blessing these turned out to be.

Later, Jo Richards moved down to Stone House where he ended his days. He is buried near the yew tree in the corner of the old yard in Felindre.

In the summer of 2001 three sisters called on me to ask about Joseph Richards and Shell Heath — Jo was their grandfather. They were Gwen, Grace and Geraldine, née Brickley. Austin also had a long talk with them as he used to live at Hope's Castle and knows quite a lot about that area.

Shell Heath has almost gone except for a few stones, so yet another little clod house bites the dust, but it has served its purpose well.

The Trefoil

This was yet another little clod house further out on the hill than Shell Heath, and this was built as a shepherd's cottage. This means that some of the farmers around would have helped to build it, in order to 'let' it to a shepherd who would look after all the sheep on the open hill.

In the 1891 census, the house was occupied by a William Pryce 35, his wife Eleanor 44, and their children, William 13, Henry 11, Ellen 7, Joseph 6, Richard 4, and Fanny 1. By the time of the 1901 census these had all moved away, but I do not know where, possibly to the Llanbadarn area, which would not be too far across the hill. I have often been amazed how, or why, these families moved so often, but with their houses so small, they could not have had much furniture and very few clothes and possessions, so a horse and cart would have been big enough, and the younger children, and maybe Mother, could have a ride too.

By 1901 Jo Richards from Shell Heath moved here with his wife Mary, daughter Martha, and a grandson, Frank Owen aged 10. This was a temporary move while Shell Heath was being rebuilt. When it was ready, Jo and his family moved back, and a Miss Hamer, The Sign, and John Price moved in. Pryce Brick, our local blacksmith, told me he used to spend his school holidays up with John Price.

The walls of this house are partly standing, but the roof has gone, so it will not be long before there will be just a few stones left.

Coventry

This is another house out on the hill beyond the Trefoil, but I can find out very little about it, or anyone living there, other than that it had quite a large area of land neatly fenced off around it — about four acres in a square. If it was a little clod house, then the builder must have been a pretty mighty fellow to have thrown the axe that far!

The modern-day phrase 'sent to Coventry' would have fitted in with this place, because you could live up there for weeks without seeing or being seen by a soul. It is not even mentioned in the census forms of 1891 or 1901, so perhaps whoever was paid to collect the forms, failed to find Coventry.

Another little place further out from Coventry was Felinwynd, but again I can find no mention of it in the census forms. Also out on the hill was a little school called The Holly Bush, and run by 'Ready Money John' — Jim the Holly Bush as he was also called. I think there are some of this family still around and I also remember hearing about the Marpoles of Holly Bush.

It was good to hear of a school in that bleak, hilly area. It meant that they were starting to form themselves into a little community, and some from up on this hill used to come down to Cwmgwyn Chapel. I have also heard that they would hold a sports day out near The Bog.

The Slopes and Cork Hall

These two little houses were built quite close together between Little House's bluebell wood and The Red Road. In 1901 William Williams 23, cowman, his wife Martha 24, and a baby daughter, possibly by the name of Brarey, but I have failed to decipher her name, aged ten months old, were living here. In addition there was a visitor, Annie Morgan, aged 16. Later on, Ned Harding moved from Hope's Castle to The Slopes where he lived for many years, still making his wiskets and baskets (and for whom see under Hope's Castle). I think he could have been the last person to live at The Slopes.

At Cork Hall in 1901 we find William Hughes 59, his wife Anne 53, and their daughter, Jessie 15. This family lived at Tynllidiart in 1891, which was just about opposite, on the other side of the road. Later, we hear about Jack Price, The Bog and his daughter, Nancy, living at Cork Hall after his wife had died. They later moved to the Lane House, but I think this family was the last to live at Cork Hall.

Both of these houses have been empty for over fifty years, and there is now no trace of either.

Wisdom Castle or Bright's Farm

This was another little clod house between Hope's Castle and Little House. I know very little about who lived there, other than that a Bright family must have lived there once to enable it to be called Bright's Farm. Later, a Thomas Owen lived there, a grandfather for Eddie Davies, Gwernerrin. This Thomas retired to the house 'up the steps' in Beguildy. I think that was where Mr. Hollins used to live. Craig, Hope's Castle, tells me that, until a few years ago, the barn was still in good shape, but it is now just about all down.

This little farm was a wet, boggy area, so, as with The Bog, the farmers around would be pleased to see it all fenced in.

The Llanbadarn area

Penybank and Cwmgarthen

Stephen and Cissy Davies moved from Blaen-Nanty in 1924 and went to Penybank, which is a large farm and farmhouse, unlike Blaen-Nanty which was once a little *ty-un-nos*. Jack was about 12 years old and his two brothers were younger. Stephen Reynolds and family moved out and Jack remembers them driving a small herd of pigs down the road, all the way to The Vron, Felindre, and what a noise they were making!

Jack told me that there were three jobs he hated doing at Penybank. One was taking the sow to the boar. They had to tie a rope to one of her legs and lead her to the farm that kept a boar, which I think was near Newtown. This was the hardest job. The second was to drive the cow to the bull, which was much easier, and the third was taking the turkey-hen to the turkey cock, but she would be put in a hessian sack and carried. All these animals would be left at the respective farms and as there were no telephones a postcard would be sent when the farmer thought they were ready to be collected, the post only being delivered every other day. So the news took a little time to travel.

Another job the young lads were expected to do was to take the eggs and butter down to Llanbadarn shop, and exchange them for the weekly groceries to then bring back home, along with a small amount of change. It was only a short distance but the boys used to ride their ponies. There were five gates to open and shut between Penybank and Llanbadarn and Jack remembered that he had once opened the one gate, when a gust of wind blew it shut and his basket of eggs went flying, so there would be no change coming home that day. This exchange of goods was one of my jobs when I was a child, but mine was a walking ticket — or a bit faster sometimes! This one day I was skipping along on the downhill singing 'Pease pudding hot, pease pudding cold, pease pudding in the pot nine days old' when over I went and my basket of eggs rolling down the hill in front of me. I returned home — a very sad little girl, with my basket of butter and a few cracked eggs in my other basket. The rest would be good food for the crows. What funny things we remember from nearly seventy years ago.

When they moved to Penybank, they continued to keep many ponies out on the open hill, but now they would winter them on some ground below Welshpool. They would round up their ponies and bring them into the fold at Penybank, check through them to see that they were all in good health, then turn them out onto the road ready for their long journey. One particular pony would always go out in front, and the rest would follow behind — with no nonsense. I think her

Left: Jack and Doris on their wedding day.
Right: Jack riding his pony with his dog by his side. He would often be carrying his gun

name was Top Lady, and no one knew why she had so much control over them. Perhaps ponies have a language all of their own, but they certainly all kept in line. Of course, there were no cars or lorries on the roads in those days. Some of the little ponies that were left on the hills did not fare so well, especially if it was a hard winter with heavy snowfalls. When the snow melted, some of these little ponies were found on the ground — frozen to death.

Jack's dad once bought a new horse-tedder from Newtown for £25, but could not pay for it that day, so Jack and his brothers, Arthur and Frank, went out and had a few good evenings rabbiting. When they had paunched and hung them, they loaded them into their old green van and took them in to Charlie's in Newtown and made £25, so they went straight away and paid dad's debt.

Cissy, their mother, was a very hard-working lady. She used to keep a lot of poultry — turkeys, ducks and chicks — and would kill and dress these all the year round. The rich people, such as the Haigs of Penithon Hall, often wanted dressed poultry for their lavish dinner parties. They would also buy eggs and butter from Penybank as well as other farms around. Jack thought that with the money Cissy was making with the poultry, eggs and butter, she was bringing in as much money as the farm was making.

Jack told me that, although his mother was a hardworking, thrifty person, she still had time to help others who were less fortunate. If she heard of a mother who was poorly, or who had just had another baby, Cissy would soon have the bread oven up to the right heat, and would bake bread, cakes and a bread or rice pudding, then the boys would have to deliver the food to that household.

In farming there was an old custom whereby if a young family moved into an unknown area, or from a smallholding into a much bigger farm, or even if it was a young couple starting out in farming, then their new neighbours would offer help to prepare the ground ready to get their three most important crops sown. These were oats for the horses in the winter; wheat to make flour for the bread to feed his family; and potatoes which were 'a must'

Jack and Prince Charles

for dinner every day. I can remember in 1938, when we moved from a smallholding up in the hills above Nantgwyn down to a large farm in the Dolau area, several of our new neighbours offered to help in this way. They would bring their own team of horses, plough a field, and prepare it ready for sowing, and then perhaps another farmer would come and sow the seeds. Some would just give half a day's work, perhaps planting potatoes, but all was gratefully accepted. Life was hard in those days, but people were always willing to help those less fortunate than themselves.

Jack married Doris Passant, a Mochdre girl, and lived at Penybank where they had their three children — Stephen, Megan and John. Arthur married May Reese from Bwlchsarnau and lived at Llanyre, whilst Frank married a local girl, May Thomas, and they lived and farmed at The Davarn, Llanbister.

Jack always supported Cwmgwyn Chapel, and even came back to the Anniversary when he was 90 years old. He had a couple of nasty accidents after that, and ended his days in a nursing home in Llandrindod. Our little Dolithon Choir used to go in and sing for them — usually old Sankey hymns. Mrs. Koreen Davies, Bwlchllyn was also in there. Jack lived to be 93 and is buried in Llanbadarn Church yard with his wife, his parents, and his son Stephen.

Stephen and his wife, Margaret, had a new house built on the same side of the road as Penybank, but just a little nearer to Llanbadarn. They have a daughter and two grandchildren. Sadly Stephen, and later Margaret, died and are buried in Llanbadarn Church yard. At the moment, Cwmgarthen is left empty. Jack's youngest son, John, still lives and farms at Penybank with his partner, Bronwen.

Dolfryn

This is a new house built in 1994 in which Erfyl Lewis, a son for Bill and Joan, The Garn, and his wife, Tracey Thomas, who is from Dolfor, live. The name Dolfryn, so I am told, means 'bottom of the meadow' and that is just where it has been built — in the bottom of Cwm-mawr meadow. Cwm-mawr was a small farm where years ago Tom and Fanny Price used to live, but it now belongs to The Garn. I think a gentleman from London now lives in the old house. Erfyl and Tracey have two children, Hannah and Bryn, and they are both at Llanbister School.

Both parents work on the farm up at The Garn, as it is here that the hub of the farming still goes on, and also most of the buildings are up there. They are both keen pony people and are especially interested in Welsh Cobs, which they show and often win prizes at Sports and Shows for miles around.

Erfyl used to sing in Cwmgwyn Chapel when he was a young lad. I remember him being one of the three kings in the Nativity play. The other two boys were our Brian and Dorrian, Alma Davies's son. They all stood up in the pulpit to sing and Erfyl, who was taller than the other two, stood in the middle. When he started to sing these two smaller boys looked up at him in awe. He must have sung better than he had at practices! Hannah sang with a group of young girls at the Centenary

Tracey, Erfyl, Hannah, Bryn, the pony, dogs and a pet ferret outside their new house — Dolfryn

Anniversary last year, so Grandma's love of music and singing still carries on down through the generations.

Last year they held a very successful Llanbadarn show and sports in the meadow by their house. I wonder what Tom and Fanny would have thought of that! It's good to see the young people taking such an interest in local events of the village. Erfyl and Tracey are also both involved in the Young Farmers' Club, especially in helping the younger members with the props for their plays and pantomimes, which they enter in the County competitions.

Tracey with Hannah and Bryn riding a Welsh cob

The Ddol Farm, Llanbadrn Fynydd

In the census of 1841 we find that Richard Bage aged 30, was living here (but no mention of a wife and family) with a Tom Pryce, who was a servant. The history of this old house at The Ddol has been of great interest to historians as it was written on parchment. The late Reg Oliver, a local historian with The Radnorshire Society, and who was also my geography master in the Grammar School in Llandrindod Wells, writes about the poet Byron. Whilst up in the Elan Valley area visiting his friend and fellow poet Shelley, he would often visit The Ddol, Llanbadarn. This must have been in the early years of the 19th century, as both these poets died before 1824 but, of course, this Richard Bage's parents could well have been living there before him.

However, in 1847 Richard Bage had a new house built at The Ddol and the old house was turned into a cowshed. He was a very learned man, a great reader, and could write well, and many came to him to ask advice on a variety of subjects. He or his family must also have been very wealthy to have built this rather splendid house and to have this plaque written above the door:

> Erected for Richard Bage
> A.D. 1847
>
> Reader
>
> What doth the Lord require of thee;
> But to do justly, and to love Mercy
> and to walk humbly with thy God.
>
> John Harding }
> John Price }   Architectives
>   T.M.

The Ddol with the plaque above the door. Olwen is in the other doorway

This reading is from the Book of Micah chapter VI, verse 8, so it would seem that he was a religious scholar. There was also a George Bage living at Cwm-mawr, so he would probably be a near relation, as there were not many Bage families around then, or now.

On the turn of the century, we see that Tom Pryce lived at The Ddol, but whether he was the servant at The Ddol in 1841, we do not know. Later, the James family lived at The Ddol and Tom Pryce, with his wife Fanny, moved to Cwm-mawr and lived there for many years. There were several of these James families around in the early 1900s. James of Gwenlas, Maesyrhelem Farm and The Garn, I think, were all related.

Some years ago, Mrs. Watson, who would be Bill Watson's mother, (and I think, would have been a granddaughter for the James family, The Ddol), told me about the Chapel Anniversaries when she was young. On Cwmgwyn Anniversary weekend, the last weekend in June, she would go home from school on the Friday, pack her best clothes and walk to The Ddol and stay with her relations that night, then on the Saturday she would walk up to The Waen and stay with another relation one night, then on Sunday she would dress in her best clothes ready for the afternoon service in Cwmgwyn. She would sing and recite, then over to Friesland for tea, back for the evening service, and then back home to Maesyrhelem Farm ready for school next day. That would have been a fair amount of exercise for one weekend, but she says she enjoyed it very much.

Now we come to the time when some of us older folk can remember. Ernie and Jane Jones were the next to live at The Ddol — Jane was one of the Reynolds' sisters who lived around Felindre. The other two sisters, Irene and Ruby, married the twin boys from The Waen, and so Jane and her children, Haydn and Julia, were often at Cwmgwyn and would take part in the Anniversaries. Haydn can remember one year he sang a duet with Erfyl, The Garn.

In 1953 Haydn married Olwen Morgan, The Farm, Beguildy, and they started their married life at The Ddol whilst Haydn's parents moved to The Bwlch Farm, Llananno. Olwen and Haydn have three children — Meudwen, Pamela and David — and they all used to come to Cwmgwyn and take part in the Anniversary, although they were brought up to go to Llanbadarn Church.

Of course, all this time, The Ddol has been a well-run farm that kept up with modern methods of farming. I think that Haydn and my husband, Doug Thomas, The Waen, were almost the first around this area to make silage, and so cut out some of the worry of haymaking in our unpredictable weather. They would work together on the silage making, and Haydn and Bert Groves, who has worked at The Ddol for a total of forty-eight years and is still there, would come over to The Waen with their forage-harvester and other machinery needed, and join Doug with our harvester, and the silage would be under cover in no time. Doug would then take our silage-making machinery down to The Ddol and together they would get The Ddol's silage in. Of course, The Ddol is a much bigger farm, so it took longer, but they worked together for several years. It was a busy time for everyone as the

Jane Jones — Haydn's mother — looking out over the snow on Christmas morning 1993

whole gang of workmen would be fed at whichever farm they were working.

In 1996 David married Linda Bennett, Trelwydan, Llanbister, and later they moved into The Ddol Farm. Haydn and Olwen now moved up to Upper Esgair — still in the Llanbadarn area. Linda and David have three children — Frances, Oliver and Charles — and these three are carrying on the tradition of singing in Cwmgwyn. In 2003 we celebrated our centenary as a Baptist chapel and these three children, together with two young Watson children, Laura and Hywel, came to sing with us. These two Watson children would be great-grandchildren for the Mrs. Watson who used to walk to Cwmgwyn many years ago, and the grandchildren for

The Jones family, the Ddol, 1995

Joan and Bill Watson, who have been joining our Cwmgwyn Choir for several years just lately. All the children from The Ddol are really from Church families, but they are very loyal and come back to Cwmgwyn to help on the Anniversary day.

Today, I hear that the modern way of farming is to go in for thousands of poultry, as well as the normal stock. We used to keep hens in deep-litter sheds and would keep around one hundred — but thousands! I'm real glad I'm on the pension!

Gwenlas

This is a very old farmhouse built around 1525, and is thought to be a 'cruck' house. These were little houses, built around a curved wooden frame and plastered with wattle and daub, which was a mixture of mud, straw and manure. These naturally curved timbers, so I have read, were similar to a shepherd's crook, and the houses were sometimes called 'crook houses'. They would have a thatched roof, and would be quite similar to our *ty-un-nos* homes, but these were built on a farmer's land, whereas the *ty-un-nos* homes were built on Crown land and had to be built and finished in one night.

Dennis, who now lives at Gwenlas, had heard that, at one time, the fire was on the centre of the floor, with a chimney going up through the room and out through

The old Gwenlas house. This picture was taken in 1889 and shows Mr. and Mrs. James with their three children and servants

the roof, but as it was built so long ago, many changes could have been made over the years. He can remember it was always a cold house and Gertie Stephens, who lived in the village and used to work at Gwenlas as well as at several other places around, used to say that it was the coldest house she had ever worked in.

Before and around the turn of the century, a Mr. and Mrs. James lived at Gwenlas with their three children and their servants. Then in around 1920, Mr. Edward Davies, The Waen, bought it and put his youngest son, John, to live there and to run the farm. John, who had had very little schooling and was still only in his early teens, and his sister, Lilla, moved into Gwenlas. I think it was a very hard life for John and a heavy responsibility for a lad of that age. I would hope that on busy times his father and brothers would help, especially at lambing and shearing and also at harvest time.

Some time later, Lilla left Gwenlas to get married to John Wilding, The Ddol. I think Mr. Edward Davies moved into Gwenlas around this time to help John. He had married Margaret Anne Jones, a widow from Blaen-Voil. Edward Davies sadly died in 1928 and his wife went back to her home in the Llanbister area to live with her mother and sister.

In 1935, John married May Hamer from Cruchel and they farmed at Gwenlas for many years. They had four children — Dennis who married Audrey from Llanbister Road; Alan who married Jackie from the New Forest and they both went back to her home to live and work. The two girls were the youngest and even before they started school, they would both ride up to The Waen — a pony each. They nearly lived on their ponies. Later, Gillian married John Thomas, a farmer's son from Dolau, and Ruth married a solicitor and judge, and they live just below Aberystwyth.

In 1948 John was made a trustee at Cwmgwyn Chapel. In 1956 when we moved to The Waen, Doug used to go down to Gwenlas most Saturday evenings to watch football and boxing on the television. We did not have electricity at The Waen, nor was the mains at Gwenlas but John, who Doug always said had a good head on his shoulders, had managed to get the old waterwheel working and it would generate enough electricity to drive the T.V. That was a grand thing as before we moved to The Waen Doug had been used to watching the telly for ten years or more. One night they had let the fire go out, and as Gwenlas was

Audrey and Dennis married in 1964

This little pony, called Loubar Showman and owned by Louise and Elaine, is a descendant of the Welsh hill ponies kept around here a hundred years ago. Here he is competing in the 6-year-old eventing championship in La Louise, France — a far cry from the coal-mines where some of his cousins would have gone. His mother still lives at Gwenlas

such a cold place to live, they began to get cold. John found an old electric fire and switched it on but — BANG — they blew the lot up!

In 1962 John had a new house built just along the road from the old one, and they all moved in and the old draughty house was left empty. John died in 1967 at the age of 77 and is buried in Maesyrhelem Chapel yard, and May is still living in her little flat in Llandrindod now aged 86.

Today Dennis and Audrey are living in the old house. It has been repaired and modernized, with central heating throughout, so they have a warm and comfortable home. Do we really appreciate all the luxuries we have in our homes today? They have three daughters — Susan, who lives in the new house, has married Andrew James, an agricultural contractor, and they farm the land, and have two little sons; Elaine is a doctor and is a partner in a practice in Llandrindod; and Louise, who works in Newtown. Neither Elaine nor Louise is married, and they both make their home with their parents. They love riding their ponies just as Gillian and Ruth had done many years before, and they now jointly own the pony Loubar Showman.

In our centenary Anniversary year, 2003, Gillian and Ruth came back to Cwmgwyn and sang a duet, and Ruth's daughter sang a solo, accompanying herself on the guitar, so music has carried on down through the generations, as both girls are the grandchildren of Mr. Edward Davies, The Waen.

Felindre Village Life

And now I would like to add just a glimpse into the village life of Felindre, where the Cwmgwyn people have always played an active part. In the early days there were three Davies brothers The Waen in the Felindre Football team and I have heard it was the best football team around. Then Arthur Brick was a very well known motor-bike rider. Later in the '70s Felindre Tug-of-War team travelled to many countries and won many cups and medals. The ladies also formed a rounders team and used to enter in the local sports around.

Then there was the Felindre W.I. When we first moved to the Waen, there was always a Cwmgwyn male voice quartet in their annual concert. Later, husbands of the W.I. members and the Cwmgwyn men would join in the singing with the ladies, and one or two brave men joined in their plays. And so the whole top end of the Teme Valley would get together — and still do — to entertain and help raise money for the W.I. and also other charities.

A postcard of Felindre sent on 16 September 1905 from 'Fanny' to a school near Rugby

Felindre Football team 1922–23
Including standing: Mr. Nicholls (schoolmaster), Jack Pugh-Morgan (son of the vicar), Arthur Galey (Anchor), Jack Morris, Mr. Brick, Jones (The Stores), Ned Davies, Tom Stephens (Cwm House), Sam Davies (carpenter), Mr. Reynolds (Rhyd-y-Cwm), Earnie Breeze, Bert Beamond, Vin Davies (the Waen)

Felindre Sports Committee about 1945
From left to right: Eddie Davies (Gwererrin), Jack Davies (Bwlch-y-llyn), Roberts (Cwmrobe), Arthur Brick with Billy Nichols just visible behind him, Ned Davies (Brickhouse) and Tom Stephens (Cwm-House)

Felindre Sports in 1922: the big parade through the village with the brass band playing. There was no village hall then, so they kept walking on down to the gate leading on to the sports field. The fancy dress would be judged just in through the gate, then it was on to the river. In the early days there was no bridge, so old Mr. Bright of Upper House used to put his four-wheeled dray in the river for people to walk across. There would be stewards at that point taking the entrance money

Arthur Brick at Kerry Sports, the first sports held after the war. His brother Pryce and Sailor Marpole are both pushing to try to get the bike started

Felindre Rounders Team in the mid 1970s

Felindre Tug-of-War team
Standing, left to right: Gilbert Reynolds (Coach), Terry Bufton, John Bevan, Llewellyn Jones, John Ellis
Seated: Gerald Davies, Roger Hughes, Robert Reynolds, Ron Woosnam, Ivor Watkins, George Williams, Edward Lloyd, Roy and David Thomas, Glyn Mills.
They travelled to Sweden, Holland, Spain, Jersey, Ireland, America and South Africa. They won a bronze medal in Switzerland in 1974 and a silver in Sweden in 1979 in the European Championships, and they won many cups and medals at both home and abroad — see the array behind the team

Ieuan Thomas and Kate Thomas of Teme Valley YFC prepare their entry for the cookery competition at the Radnor Federation County rally at Clyro

Teme Valley YFC members presenting their carol-singing donations to the Air Ambulance Charity

Our new village hall opened in 1949. This made life much easier for the clubs and other organizations in the village. Before it was built, the W.I. used to use the chapels or Crug-y-Byddar School, where one year while they were all on stage, the whole lot collapsed — singers and stage

Snow White and the Seven Dwarves — a W.I. concert in the early 1970s. From left to right: Brian Thomas, Paul Barrett, Stephen Reynolds, Stephen Barrett, Rozalind Lakelin, Christopher Barrett, Megan Matthews, William Johnson, Yvonne Reynolds, Christine Lloyd, Carlton Brick, Steph Lakelin

A Christmas Party, with John Stephens as Frosty and Geoff Horn as the Fairy

Our gypsy scene. Bryan would be in the hall for days painting the scenery

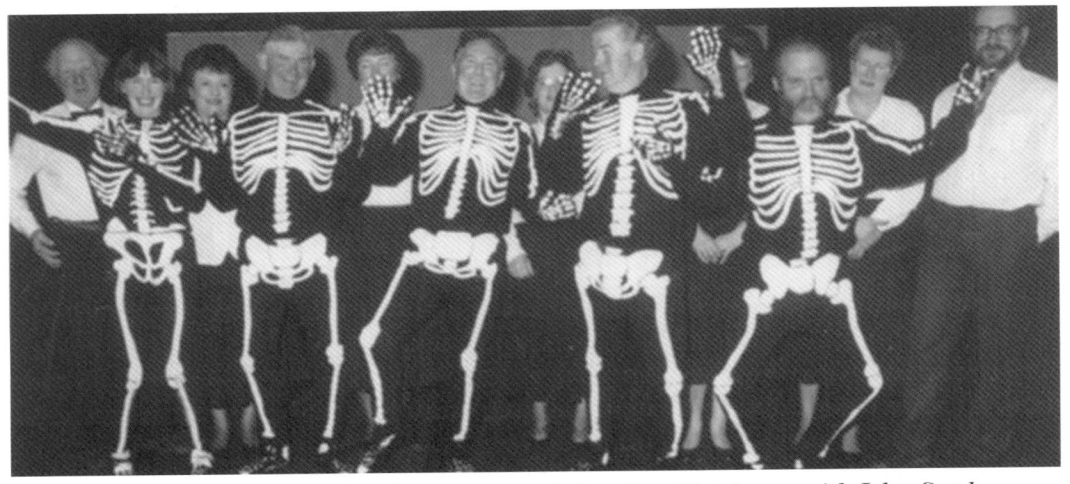

Dem Bones Dem Bones. Our brave men and Caroline Matthews, with John Stephens and Keith Thomas on either side and the ladies hiding behind

The ladies fighting over Bryan and Shirley Bright 'trying to keep the peace'

The Young Farmers always take part in the W.I. concert. Here our cowboys are singing round the camp fire. Standing: Robert Thomas, Rebe Brick, John Thomas. Sitting: Dianne Lewis, Megan Matthews, Monica Thomas, Janet Lewis, Jean Reynolds

My retirement from teaching.
What a surprise when I arrived at school. I had thought it was going to be just my class and their parents to watch our little play, but the yard was full of folk. It was just as well that I didn't know what was coming

Mr. McGregor has had enough of his garden. I am trying to lift some of the young ones down from the platform

The hall was packed with parents and friends. I am trying to encourage the children to sung louder. What a face!

Maggie had handed me a packet, but I noticed it was an air ticket so I handed it back. Here Maggie tries again whilst Geoff Duthie assures me that it is meant for me. Moira is shouting 'take it — its for you'. Wow! It was a ticket for a two hour trip on Concorde. What a valley and what a school. Thanks to everyone who must have given so generously

Index

Where extensive details of a family are given the index entry has been made to that family linked to the property in which they live(d). Individuals are otherwise mentioned, again often linked to the name of a property to aid identification. Entries in italics refer to photographs.

Archie the Drover *3*, 5

Bage family (The Ddol, Llanbadarn Fynydd) 161-162
Baker, Mrs. *viii*
Banks, John Shaw 16
Barnett family *30*, *31*, *32*
    Bill (The Rhuvid) *32*
    Rhona (The Rhuvid) 76
Barrett family *31*, *32*
    Barbara & George 129, 151
    David 95
Beguildy School 40
Benbow family (Prysg) 116
Bibbs, Mr. & Mrs. G. 14
Birkenhead, earl of 6-7
Blaen-cwm-Voil 100, 104
Blaen-Nanty 105-108, *109*
Blaen-Voil 100, 104
Bliss family (Lower Voil) 101
Bog, The 152-153
Botwood family (Newcwm) 145
    Teddy (the Nanty) 111, 114-115, *114*
Bowen family (The Waen) 49-50
    John (The Mines) 17
Brick, Arthur & Blodwyn *23*, 24, *25*, *25*, 61, 104, 131, 167, *168*, *169*
    Elsie 4
    Rebe *60*
    Vaunda *43*, *52*
Brickhouse (Bryn-Mawr) 74, 78-80, *79*
Bridge, Rev. John 24
Bright, Aaron 152
Brights' Farm 156
Brown family (Newcwm) 148
Bufton, Mr. Walter 123-124
Butterwell 96-100, *97*, 109
Bwlch-y-llyn 42, 44-47, *46*
Byron, Lord 161

Campbell, Alwena & Charles (Prysg) *viii*, 8, 27, 86, 117
Charles, Prince *85*, *158*
Chatterley, Dorothy & Michael 46
Cider House 1, 2-3, 11-14, *12*, *13*
Corbett, family *31*

Cork Hall 87, 155-156
Coventry 155
Coyle, Richard 'Green Wellies' *4*
Crewe family (The Culvert) 42
Criggin, The 53
Crug-y-Byddar School 37, *38*, 39, *43*
Culvert, The 41-42
Cwm-Nanty 115
Cwmgarthen 156-159
Cwmgwyn Chapel 14-33
Cwmgwyn Cottage 33
    Hall 85-86

Danes 59-62, *60*, *61*, *62*
Davies family (Blaen-Nanty) 12, 105
    family (Blaen-Cwm-Voil) 104
    family (Bwlch-y-llyn) 45-47
    family (Cider House) 13
    family (The Ddol) 51, 52-53
    family (Dolfrynog) 37-39, *37*
    family (Penfynon) 113
    family (The Turgey) 143
    family (The Waen) 50-54
    Mrs. (Dolfor) *18*
    Albert (The Gwridd, Anchor) 69
    Alma *23*
    Bill (The Garn) *32*, *102*
    Billy (The Green) 114
    Denise & Fred (Dolfrynog & Butterwell) 97
    Dennis & Audrey & family 165, *165*, 166, *166*
    Dorothy (Brickhouse) *18*
    Eddie (Gwererrin) *168*
    Edward (Brickhouse) 22, 78, *78*
    Edward (The Waen) 15-16, *15*, *16*, 17, 18, 19, 21, 27, 50-51, 104, 165
    Evan 3
    Frank (Dafern) 35
    Fred (Bryn Picca, Mochdre) 13, 35
    Glen *23*
    Irene 51, 53, 78, *78*
    Jack (Bwlch-y-llyn) *168*
    Jack & Doris (Blaen-Nanty/Penybank) 4, *4*, 12, 19, 105-6, *106*, 156-159, *157*
    James & Elizabeth (The Lluest) 139-142, *140*

James (Windy Hall) 14
John (Bwlch-y-llyn) 17, 99
John & May (Gwenlas) 22, *35*, 53-54, *53, 104*, 165, 166
John Easson (Bwlch-y-llyn) 22, *23*, 45, *45*, 46, 47
Joyce (The Waen) *43*, 52, *52*
Koreen *23,* 45, *45*, 46, 47
Lilla (The Ddol) *35*, 36, 51, 52-53, 165
Mary (Butterwell) 96-97
Mervyn & Bronwen (Blaen-Nanty) 107
Myfanwy *129*
Mylton 142
Ned & Vin (The Waen) 51-52
Richard 99
Ruby *23*
Sidney (The Waen) 50, 51
Stephen (Blaen-Nanty) 12, 17
Stephen & Margaret 159
Ddol (Cwmgwyn) 8, 33-36
Ddol (Lanbadarn Fynydd) 161-164, *161*
Deakin, Sue (Howey) 59
Devannor 15
Dobson, Rev. Stuart 95
Dolfryn 159-160, *160*
Dolfrynog 8, 37-41, *40*, 73, 140
Dolithon Choir 59
Drovers 2-5
Duthrie, George & Carolyn & family 119-120

Edward family (Tynllwyn) 120
Edwards, Colin 41
emigration 49
Evans family (Hafod Fadog) 83
family (Llethrau Cottage) 123
family (Lower Voil & Upper Llaithddu Farm) 101
family (Prysg) 116
Rev. James 83
Lily (Cwmdolfu) 39
Paul *129*
Ron & Anne (Fiddlers Green) 74, 79
Trevor (Lower Voil) 101, *102*
Walter (Knucklas) 24

Felindre Sports *168, 169*
Felinwyndd 155
Fiddlers Green 70-76, *74*
football teams 167, *168*
Foot & Mouth 65-66
Foster, Nelda *viii*
Fountain Farmers 126

Frances, Horace & Muriel & family (Tynllwyn) 122
French family (Fiddlers Green) 75, *75*
Friesland House 19, 81

Galey, Arthur *168*
Gardner, Andrew & Karen & family 130
Garman, Dr. 94
Garn, The 110-113, 159
George (The Hendy) 19
John & Elsie 135-136, *136*
Richard *32*
Richard, Betty & Gilbert *133*
Sid & Elsie 124-125, *125*, 126
Gerrard, Mrs. 10-11
Gomm, Mrs 148
Goodman, Bert *43*
Bill 150
Gorther (Mill) 83
Gough, Glithyn 127
Richard & Dorothy 128, 138
Gravel, The 81-83
Greenall, Elsie 70-72
Griffiths, Don 18, 70, 78
Edwin (Devannor) 15
Rev. Hubert Vavasour 15, 34, 81, 130
Jane 70
R. (Coed-y-Hendre) 15
Thomas (Cwmgrenglin) 15
W. 15
Groves, Bert 162
Gwenlas 58, *58*, 164-166, *164*
Gwilt, Mr. R. (Llanfair Waterdine) 17

Hafod Fadog 35, 83-84
Hall, Robin 152
Halsey, Michael & Claudi *103*
Hamer family (Bwlch-y-llyn) 44
Miss (Shell Heath) 155
Miss (Blaen-Nanty) 107-108
Henry (The Turgey & The Oaks) 143
Rev. J.D. 15
Jack & Mary (Polly) & family (High Park) 135, *135*, 136, *136,* 137
John (High Park) 22
Harding family (The Bog) 152
Edward 149, 150, 155
Hardwick, Joyce (Llaithddu) 59
Harris family *30*, *31*, *32*
Tom 118, 122, 123, 136
Hart, Robert *30*
Haynes, Effie 88

Higgins, Charlie & Jessie 154
High Park 135-137, *136*
Hobbs, Denise 76
Holly Bush Jim 155
Holly Bush School 155
Holmes, Mrs. Elizabeth 126, *126*
Hope's Castle 8, 149-152, *149*
Horne, Ron & Judy 148
Horton, Rev. Thomas 17
Hudson, Mrs. Dorothy (Cow Hall) 70
Huffer, E., Neville, Thomas & Eric *129*
    Margaret *23*
Hughes family (Tynllidiart & Cork Hall) 87, 155-156
    family (Cwm-Nanty) 115
    Mr. T.D. 18
Humphreys, Sarah 48

Jack of Cork 56
James family (Cwmllechwyd) 110
    family (Gwenlas) 164, *165*
    Beatie 72, *73*
    Clifford (Cwmgwyn) *viii*, 24, 25, *42*, *43*
    Clifford (Fiddlers Green) 69, 72-73, *73*
    Dorothy *32*
    Rev. J. (The Culvert) 15, 16, 41
    J. (The Garn) 17
    James (The Garn) 110, *110*
    Jim (Thomas) *23*, 72, *73*
    Kate Naomi 72, *73*
    Martha (The Garn) 111
    Thomas & Laura (Fiddlers Green) 19, 72, *73*
    Tom & Laurie (Walk Mill & Fiddlers Green) 39, 134
    Tom *56*
Jones family (Blaen-cwm-Voil) 104
    family (Cider House) 12
    family (The Ddol, Llanbadarn Fynydd) 162-163, *163*
    family (High Park) 135
    family (Persandy) 142
    family (Slate House) 137
    family (Windy Hall) 67-69
    Mr. & Mrs. (teachers at Beguildy School) 90
    Abraham (Windy Hall) 15-16, *15*, *16*, 17, 18, 19, 22, 27, 50-51, 67-68, *67*, *68*, *69*, 70
    Barbara *129*
    Brenda *102*, 102-103
    Cissy (Cider House) 12
    Doris (Windy Hall) *69*
    Doug (Dutlas) 21
    Emrys 102-103, *102*
    Ethel (Windy Hall) 69
    Henry & Mary & family (Medwaledd) 128
    Ivor *42*
    Jack (Windy Hall) 68, *69*
    Kitty (Fiddlers Green) 42
    Lynn M.P. & Chris *98*, 99, 100
    Morley 114
    Pryce & Joan & family (Kerry) 133-134
    Reuben 22
    Rhys & Elsie & family (Lower Voil) 102-103
    Ray *43*
    Sarah (Windy Hall) 67, 68, 70
    Trevor (Windy Hall) *42*, *43*

King's Rent, The 153
Knighton Cubs 21-22
knitting 98, 99
Knowles, Sir Francis Howe Seymour 115

Lakelin, Mr. 153
Lambourne, Wendy & David 24, *29*
lead mine 125
Leason family (Fiddlers Green) 74-75
Lees, Mr. 100-101
Lewis family (Blaen-Nanty) 107, 108
    family (The Gravel) 81-83
    family (Llethrau Cottage) 122
    family (Panty-Beudy) 118
    Bill & Joan (Blaen-nanty) 111, 112, *112*, 113
    Emrys *43*
    Erfyl & Tracey 112, *112*, 159, 160, *160*
    Fred 53
    J.E. (Hafod Fadog) 17
    Joan *viii*, *18*, *29*
    John (The Gravel) 17, 82, 83
    John & Jane (Bwlch-y-llyn) 45, 81, 83
    Margaret (Criggin) *viii*, 19, *23*, *29*, *69*, *102*
    Nancy (The Garn) 112, 113
    Pryce 124
    Rene *23*
    Thelma 112, *112*
    Tom & Alice (Blaen-Nanty) 107
    Wynford & Robin (Springfield) 108, 109, *109*
Little House 8, 87-96, *92*, *94*
Llanmadoc 8
Llethrau 85, 88, 123-127
    Cottage 8, 81, 122-123
Lloyd family (High Park) 135
    family (Hope's Castle) 150

      family (Llethrau) 123-124, 126, 142
      Mr. & Mrs. (Crochen) 89
      Edward 43, *43*
      George & William (The Culvert) 42-43, *42*
      Iris *42*, *68*
      Ray (Knighton) 25
      Sybil *42*
      Mr. W. (High Park) 17
Lluest, The 139-142
Lower Fiddlers Green *62*, 76-78, *77*
Lower Voil 100-103, *101*

Mansfield, Rev. W.G. 15, 16, 17, 18, 27
Mantle family (Little House) 87
      Clarice & Freda 13
Manuel, William (Bwlchsarnau) 24, 27, 44
Martin family (Panty-Beudy) *117*, *118*, 118-119
Mapole, Clifford *43*
      Johnny 19
      William 14
McCann, Bryan & Gwyneth *viii*, 24, 25, *29*, 52, 76-78, *77*, *78*, 79, *80*
      Marcia 36, 79
Medwaledd 126, 127-130, *128*
Meredith family *31*, *32*
      Agnes 146
      Hannah *viii*, *133*
Meredith-Powell, Mr. 24
Mills, Mrs. (Medwaledd) 18
      John & Myfannwy & family (Little House, Llethrau & Medwaledd) 22, 87-88, 124, 129-130, 142
Moody, Dwight L. 20-21
Morgan family (Brickhouse) 78
      family (Fiddlers Green) 71-72
      family (Llethrau Cottage) 122
      Betty 13
      Charlie, Sarah & family (The Prysg) 116-117
      George *30*
      Naomi & Richard (Fiddlers Green) 39, 71-72, 105
      'Red' Tom 154
      Reuben (Fiddlers Green) 17, 27, *69*, *71*
      Reuben (Little House) 19, 87
      Richard (The Prysg) 115
Morris family (Brickhouse) 78
      Arthur (Brickhouse) 17
      David & Frances *viii*, 24, 25, *29*
      Frances (Pound Gate) *29*, 76
      Jack *168*
      Les (Wharf Inn) 139

Nesbitt, John 97
Newcwm 145-148, *147*
Newhouse / The Nest 146
Nicolls, Mr. (Llandewi) 92
Norman, Mrs. 14

Oaks, The 143-144, *144*
Old Carpenter's Shop (Dutlas) 121, *121*
Old House, Bwlch-y-llyn 6
Owen, Thomas 156

Page, Rev. I.E. 14
Panty-Beudy 117-120, *117*, *118*, *119*
Parker, Edward (The Waen) 47
Penfynon 113
Penithon Hall 45
Penlington, David & Jayne 122, 136
Penybank 107, 156-159
Peregrine, John 27, *41*, *95*
Perks Rhoss 130
Persandy 142
Powell, Andrew & Thelma 112
Prest, Mr. 132
Price family (The Bog) 152-153
      family (The Waen) 48
      Albert & Tilda (Newcwm) *23*, 147-148, *147*
      Bill (Buckle) & Jenny (Butterwell) 99, *99*
      J. & T. 15
      John (Cork Hall) 134
      John (Shell Heath) 155
      John (The Waen) 48
      Ken *viii*
      Tilda *viii*, *23*
Prisoners of War 124, 128, 142
Pritchard, Mr. & Mrs. Ron 41
Pryce family (The Oaks) 143
      family (Panty-Beudy) 118
      family (The Trefoil) 154-155
      Anne (The Prysg) 115
          Martha (The Garn) 111
Prysg, The 8, 115-117, *116*
Pugh family (Blaen-Voil / Slate House) 104
      family (Slate House) 137-139, *138*
      family (The Turgey / The Bog) 143, 144, *144*
      Arthur 144
      Clifford & Olwen & family 121, *121*
      David Thomas (Slate House) 22
      George (Slate House) 22
      Gilbert (Slate House) 17, 22, *23*, 24
      Jack (The Bog / Cork Hall) 156
      James & Eliza (Medwaledd) 17, 127-128, *127*
      Layton *102*

    Lily (Slate House) 42
    Maggie *97*, 104, *104*, 107, 138
    Noel *102*
    Victor & Lucy & family (Tynllwyn) 120-121, *120*
    William Pryce (Slate House) 22
Pugh-Morgan, Jack *168*

Rees, Garfield 45
Reese, Miss *43*
Reid-Macintosh Associates 95
Reynolds family (The Oaks) 143-144
    family (Walk Mill) 36, 37
    Charlie *31*
    Dora 36
    Elizabeth (Llaithddu) 35
    Ella 35
    Irene 51-52, 72, 78, *78*
    Iris (The Vron) (see also Wilding) 9-10, 133
    John (Rhyd-y-Cwm) *35*
    Kate *31*
    Phoebe 4, 98
    Ruby 51-52, *52*, 72
    Ruth (Rhyd-y-Cwm) *35*
    Sam 72
    Tom (Llanllwyd) 53
    William 36
Richards family (Hope's Castle / Medwaledd) 128, 129, 150-152, *150*, *151*
    family (Shell Heath / The Trefoil) 154, 155
    Rev. & Mrs. L.M. *23*, 136
    Frank (Lane House) 95
Roberts, Christopher & Robin (The Forge) 25
    John *43*, 95
    Owen & Freda & family (Blaen-Nanty) 108, *108*
roads 7
Rogers, Mr. (Gwernerrin) 51
rounders team 167, *170*
Rowlands, Thomas & Sarah 101

St. David 96
Sanford, John & Sarah 80
Sankey, Ira D. 2-21
Savage, Margaret 22
    Megan *viii*, *29*, *102*, 103
Scott, Gerald & Dorothy 44, 52, *69*, 79, *80*
Shaw family (Brickhouse) 80
Shell Heath 154
Simons 114
Sinclair, Andy 76
Slate House, The 137-139

Slopes, The 155-156
Spillsbury, Mr. & Mrs. 74, 76, *77*
Springfield 109, *109*
Stanfield, Mable *viii*
Stephens family (Cwmgwyn Hall) 85-86
    Aggie 92
    Alwena (see Campbell)
    Bill *114*, 115
    Burton 22, 85
    Mr. C. (Cwmgwyn Hall) 17
    Charles & Una 35, 84
    Ella 20
    George & Jane 86, 91
    Gertie 165
    John (Older) 18, *18*
    John (The Hall) & Margaret *viii*, 19, 22, 23, *23*, 25, *85*, 86, *86*, 93, *104*
    John (Youngest) & Mair (Hafod Fadog) *viii*, 26, *26*, 76, 84, *84*, 86
    Martin (Hafod Fadog) 22, *23*
Stoney Pound 4
Stores, The 132, 139
Swindler, Bill 10

Thomas family (The Waen) *viii*, *31*, *32*, 54-67, *54*, *56*, *58*, *63*
    Brian & Yvonne & family *63*, 65, *65*
    David & Jackie & family *viii*, *63*, 63-64, 65-66, 79
    Dianne & Robert & family 25, *63*, 65, *65*
    Doug & Clarice 22, *23*, 25, 27, 79-80, 113, *114*, 162, *175*, *176*
    Graham Maureen & Evan 64, *64*
    Gethyn *31*
    Ieuan *31*
    John & Frances & family 64, *64*
    Keith *viii*, *28*, *29*
    Meredith (The Stores) 139
    Morris (Newtown) 95
    Robert & Karen 64, *64*
Trefoil, The 154-155
tug-of-war team 167, *170*
Turf & Knife Tax 153
Turgey, The 50, 143
Turner, Richard & Janet 122
Ty-un-nos 5-8
Tyn-y-Cwm 34, 130-134, *131*
Tynllidiart 86-87, 155
Tynllwyn 8, 120-122

Vallance, Philip (Little House) 24, 94-95
    Wendy 95, *95*

'Victory Houses' 152
Village Hall *172*

Waen, The 47-67
Walk Mill 36-37, *36*
Watkins, Gareth *31*
Watson family 163-164
    Bill (Maesyrhelen) *viii*, 19, 24
Webster, George & Lesley (Newcwm) *43*, 145-146
Weiss, Mr. & Mrs. 122-123
Welsh Hill ponies 106
Whittall family (Tyn-y-Cwm) 130
Wilding family (The Ddol) 13, 33-36, *34*, *35*
    family (Tyn-y-Cwm) 130-138
    Bert 132, *133*
    Dora *34*, 36
    Ella 34, *34*, 35
    George 24, 25
    Iris 131, 132-133, *132*
    Joan 131, 132, 133
    John (The Ddol) 36, 52-53
    Lilla 18
    Marcia (The Ddol) 76
    Mary (Tyn-y-Cwm) *viii*, 19, *43*, 131, 132, 133, 134
    Mary Anne 13, 34, *34*, 35

Pryce 17, 34, *34*
Pryce Stephen 34, *34*, 35
Thomas 134
Una 34, *34*, 35
Williams family (Hope's Castle) 149
    family (The Slopes) 155
    family (Walk Mill / Newcwm) 37, *145*, 146-147
    family (Yrchyn) 9
    Bert *32*
    Edward & Mary (Friesland) 81
    Frances *viii*, *31*
    Olwen *43*
    Pryce Richard 146-147
Windy Hall 67-70, *69*, 140
Wisdom Castle 156
Wishart, Rev. M. *41*
Wooley family (Blaen-Nanty) 107
Woosnam family (Simons) 114
Womens Institute 167, *172*, *173*, *174*
Wyke, Mr. & Mrs. (Fiddlers Green) 75

Yorke, Sue & Stephen 126
Young Farmers Club 110, *171*, *174*
Yrchyn/Yr-ychen 1, 9-11, *10*, *11*